SCRAPBOOKING
YOUR FAMILY HISTORY

MAUREEN A. TAYLOR

BETTERWAY BOOKS

CINCINNATI, OHIO

SCRAPBOOKING
YOUR FAMILY HISTORY

ABOUT THE AUTHOR

Maureen A. Taylor (www.taylorandstrong.com) is the author of several books and articles on genealogy and photo history, including *Preserving Your Family Photographs* (Betterway Books, 2001), and *Uncovering Your Ancestry Through Family Photographs* (Betterway Books, 2000). She is also the author of *Through the Eyes of Your Ancestors* (Houghton Mifflin, 1999), a basic guide to family history for kids. She is a contributing editor at *Family Tree Magazine* and is a former picture research coordinator and photo curator. Maureen's numerous television and radio appearances include *The View*, *MSNBC* and *DIY: Scrapbooking*.

Scrapbooking Your Family History. Copyright © 2003 by Maureen A. Taylor. Manufactured in China. All rights reserved. No part of this book may be reproduced in any form or by any electronic or mechanical means including information storage and retrieval systems without permission in writing from the publisher, except by a reviewer, who may quote brief passages in a review. Published by Betterway Books, an imprint of F&W Publications, Inc., 4700 East Galbraith Road, Cincinnati, Ohio 45236. (800) 289-0963. First edition.

Other fine Betterway Books are available from your local bookstore or direct from the publisher.

07 06 05   5 4 3 2

Cataloging-in-Publication data is available from the Library of Congress at <http://catalog.loc.gov>.

ISBN 1-55870-683-6

Editors: Sharon DeBartolo Carmack and Jerry Jackson Jr.
Cover and Interior Designer: Joanna Detz
Interior Layout Artist: Karla Baker
Production Coordinator: Sara Dumford
Photographer: Al Parrish
Photo Stylist: Mary Barnes Clark

With every book, there are people to thank. My editor, Sharon Carmack, guided me through three books and suggested I pursue freelance writing. To Lynn, Jane, and Michele—three friends and former colleagues who have read countless versions of articles and books—THANK YOU! Together the four of us have spent hours in craft and scrapbook stores trying out new products and even buying them. Michele Leinaweaver and Diane Haddad edited chapters and offered solutions. Diane also created the sample pages that appear in the text. So many suppliers contributed products for inclusion that it's impossible to thank them all. However, there are a couple of special individuals who talked me through a few steps including: Lynn Morgan of Anna Griffin, Inc., Lynn Kordus of Fiskars, Marianne Elizabeth Schwers of Vintage and Vogue, and Sally Queen of Sally Queen Associates. Tim Salls and Chad Leinaweaver helped find illustrations and lent material from their institutions, the New England Historic Genealogical Society and the New Jersey State Historical Society.

Portions of this book have appeared elsewhere including *Memory Makers Magazine*, *Family Tree Magazine*, and *New England Ancestors* (print and online). The photo permission section in Chapter 2 appeared in *Writer's Digest* (September 2001) as "Free Art? Not So Fast" co-authored with Sharon DeBartolo Carmack. Some of the material is updated and revised from my earlier books, *Uncovering Your Ancestry Through Family Photographs* (Betterway Books, 2000) and *Preserving Your Family Photographs* (Betterway Books, 2001).

I especially have to thank my children, James and Sarah, who continually surprise me with their support. Sarah always comes up with an innovative way to use the scrapbook projects I bring home. She even has an interest in "ancestors" while her brother likes to hear about how earlier generations lived. Of course, there wouldn't be books or articles without the encouragement of my patient husband. Dexter, James, and Sarah—thank you for letting me have the best room in the house as an office.

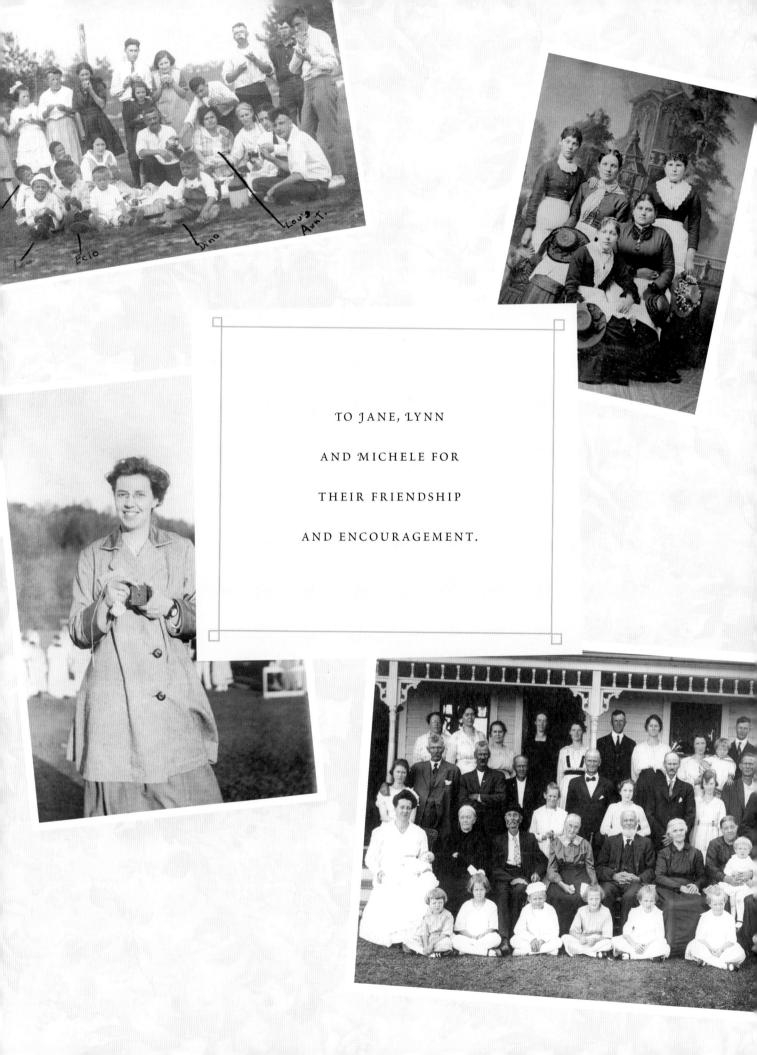

TO JANE, LYNN

AND MICHELE FOR

THEIR FRIENDSHIP

AND ENCOURAGEMENT.

TABLE OF CONTENTS

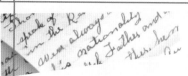

PREFACE

I can't deny it. I'm fascinated with artistic expressions of family history from antique photographs to quilts, and this interest extends to today's heritage albums. Each of these items includes visual information and family history. I believe that genealogy is a hobby for everyone that can be expressed in a variety of formats from family trees to published books. Heritage albums and other family history crafts are worth every second you spend putting them together because they are a legacy for future generations. It's important to pass that family history on to our children so they feel more comfortable with themselves as they become adolescents and adults. Genealogy helps children understand their role in the family. This is true for all types of families, from the traditional two-parent unit to adoptive families and everything in between. What better way to share family stories than with the words and pictures combined in a hand-crafted heritage album?

This book is for scrapbookers who want to create a family history album and for family historians who want to interpret their discoveries and bring their ancestors to life in a heritage album. I hope this book encourages scrapbook enthusiasts to put more family history in their heritage albums and that it encourages genealogists to create heritage scrapbooks. While genealogy and history are cousins because they cover the same ground, it is important to realize that heritage albums are also part of the same family tree. Scrapbooking and genealogy are both hobbies that have seen dramatic growth in the past few years. According to a survey released at the 2002 Hobby Industry Association Convention & Trade Show, sales of scrapbook supplies in the last five years skyrocketed from $200 million in 1997 to $1.4 billion in January 2002.

Likewise in 2000, Maritz Marketing and Genealogy.com discovered that sixty percent of the population was interested in family history, up from forty-five percent in 1995. Not surprisingly, there are scrapbookers interested in genealogy and vice versa. The number of people who create heritage albums is large enough to support multiple publications and specialty products.

Whether you create a scrapbook page of a single event or an album of your entire heritage, you are still scrapbooking your family history. In order to inject a little family history into your pages and albums, you'll need to know where to begin. This book will show you how to put family history in your scrapbook by:

• Explaining how to trace your family tree.

• Showing you how to locate new materials—photographs, documents, memorabilia, and artifacts—to enliven your pages.

• Helping you organize and care for your treasure trove of material.

• Explaining how to understand family history through the materials you've located.

• Teaching you safe scrapbooking techniques to preserve what you create for the future.

• Using the history of the development of photographs, scrapbooks, and manuscripts to help you identify materials to include in your family history.

Genealogies tell the story of a family in documents, words, and pictures, similar to the way a scrapbook does, but in a more complex fashion.

Scrapbooks are not intended to include the amount of detail contained in a published genealogy. Instead, a scrapbook's purpose is to tell the tale in words and pictures anyone can understand. Women (and some men) have been creating art that features genealogy for centuries: signature quilts, watercolor family trees, needle-work samplers, and scrapbooks. These beautiful and personal creations are artifacts as well as family history. Perhaps you've thought of creating a lasting record of your genealogy, but don't know where to begin. It's easy—you start with yourself and work backwards. As you delve into the past you'll get hooked by "the genealogy bug" due to unexpected and thrilling discoveries.

Each chapter builds on the information you learned in the previous one through:

- Skill-building exercises
- Profiling new sources of genealogical material
- Extensive illustrations to show and tell
- Hands-on tutorials
- Terminology
- Additional resources to help you learn more about a topic

This book also explains the following steps in creating a heritage album:

- Researching family history (starting the search)
- Gathering materials (photographs, manuscripts, and memorabilia)
- Learning about social history (using resources such as people, libraries, and the Internet)
- Finding different ways to tell the story (captioning and charts)
- Defining a focus (planning, sorting, layout, and purchasing supplies)
- Organizing what's left over (proper storage techniques)
- Creating a heritage album that will last (safe scrapbook materials and techniques)
- Delving further into family research (more ways to find family)

PUTTING THE HERITAGE IN YOUR SCRAPBOOK

So why take the time to create a scrapbook? Unlike a published genealogy, a scrapbook is meant to be viewed repeatedly, like a photo album. You will need to conduct research and purchase some special scrapbook supplies, but especially use what you have at hand. Ultimately, your goal is to put your family history together in a visual and informational presentation. The time you take to pull together relevant materials and the money spent will be appreciated for generations. There are many different ways, from expensive to inexpensive, to accomplish the same goal. A variety of low-cost alternatives for budget-conscious scrapbookers are offered in each chapter.

The current fascination with scrapbooks is nothing new. While it's unknown how old this hobby actually is, scholars trace its origins to the seventeenth century when notes and prints were kept in albums. In the nineteenth century, "scrap" referred to colorful bits of paper that included product labels and greeting cards as well as some specialty papers created just for the scrapbook craze of the Victorian era. No one was immune to the lure of the scrapbook. Men, women, and children compiled scrapbooks using blank books or creating handmade ones from cloth or paper. They collected friendship mementos and paper memorabilia that were part of their daily lives. Some scrapbooks resembled journals, while others kept track of occurrences, quotes, recipes, knitting swatches, and anything else an individual was interested in. Both the look and the purpose of scrapbooks has changed over the centuries.

Let's take a brief look at the history of the medium and some ways to interpret and care for the albums in your family. After seeing how older albums were put together, you might decide to use some of those techniques in your own heritage album. I've also included suggestions on how to find ancestral scrapbooks.

Thomas Jefferson kept scrapbooks filled with newsclippings like this one. His albums are at his former home in Charlottesville, Virginia. Courtesy of Monticello/Thomas Jefferson Foundation.

COMMON-PLACE BOOKS

Educated men and women pasted quotes and phrases in things they called common-place books. Thomas Jefferson gathered newspaper articles of his presidency in his leather-bound volumes of plain paper. He also included clippings, drawings, and diary entries. By the first half of the nineteenth century, albums like his featured embossed covers, engraved clasps, and locks. They became a cross between a scrapbook and a journal. Hattie Harlow of Boston, a seamstress, organized her notes, clippings, and illustrations by topic in separate handmade volumes with wallpaper and cardboard covers. One of her common-place books even includes knitting samples with directions.

GRANGER BOOKS

Building on the popularity of common-place books, in 1769 William Granger introduced a printed book with extra blank pages for the owner to personalize with autographs, letters, or illustrations relating to the subject of the publication. For instance, a Granger book on the history of London could be embellished with clippings of appropriate illustra-

tions, travel notes, and even plant samples. Early scrapbookers began imitating the Granger book style by adding pages to existing publications. There were even manuals that described how to "extra illustrate" a book. These types of books are difficult to locate in library collections because they are usually filed under the author of the book, not under the name of the person who embellished the volume.

FRIENDSHIP ALBUMS

Young women in the Victorian period often created memory books or visitor albums filled with signatures, scrap, cards, hair, handwriting, poetry, and even photographs of their family and friends. These could be shared and added to whenever someone came to visit. These friendship albums expanded on the concept of autograph books that had originated in Germany in the seventeenth century by incorporating traditions of Victorian female friendships such as collecting hair weavings or swapping friendship tokens. Laura L. Sherwin of Fairhaven, Vermont, for example, donated a piece of hair for Hellen M. Adams's friendship album.

SCRAPBOOKS

A scrapbook is a collection of any type of material pasted into an album, but historically it consisted of paper materials, photographs, and memorabilia. Scrapbooking peaked in the nineteenth century between 1880 and 1890, when a popular manual on the topic became available. The colorful scraps, known as ephemera, gathered in scrapbooks during the nineteenth century were meant to be disposable, not collectible. While these albums contain an assortment of material accumulated as compiler's went through their daily routines, some "scrap" was purchased expressly for the albums. Scrap manufacturers created a demand for their product by offering sheets in new styles directed at women and children, much like the advertisers in today's scrapbook periodicals. Contemporary women's magazines featured numerous articles on the

> **Heritage Album Tip:**
>
> *Make your own scrapbook using cloth covers and special papers—such as vellum or parchment—or use a journal with acid- and lignin-free paper.*

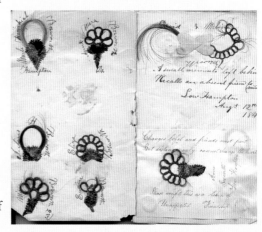

Hellen M. Adams's Friendship Album that included hair samples, autographs, and quotes from family and friends. New England Historic Genealogical Society.

value of scrapbooks as a family activity and educational tool, thus encouraging novices to learn about scrapbooking.

Just as today's scrapbooks have themes, earlier generations of scrapbook enthusiasts also created albums for a variety of purposes. Housewives kept the labels and trade cards from new consumer products and included them in their albums, while college students documented their years at school. In fact, if you can't find a scrapbook created by an ancestor and you know he or she attended a particular college, contact the special collections department at that institution to see if there is one compiled by a classmate. Who knows? It might feature a photograph or autograph of your ancestor. At the very least, you'll discover details about their college experience.

Just like today, scrapbooking was a hobby for anyone. Ordinary citizens and even President Rutherford B. Hayes spent time adding to their scrapbooks. Mark Twain was such an avid scrapbooker that he reserved Sundays for his hobby. He held patents for his invention of self-pasting scrapbooks that could be dampened with water. By 1901, at least fifty-seven different types of Mark Twain albums were available. Albums could also be purchased from the Montgomery Ward catalog, but many individuals created their own albums. Due to a book shortage during World War II, Books Across the Seas, a book exchange program, sponsored a scrapbook exchange between students in England and the United States. These albums, worked on as group projects, focused on local history and student life.

Scrapbooks can reveal the lives of their compilers through the type of items pasted onto the pages and their arrangement. Some hobbyists used their albums as a form of artistic expression. One scrapbooker dressed

"A Tribute of Love" Piece of scrap with an unidentified man's photograph. Collection of the author.

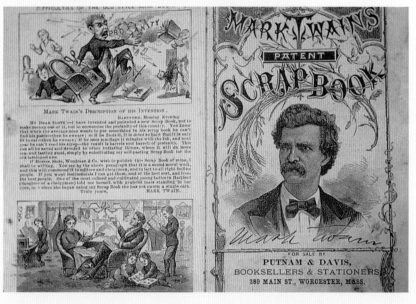

Mark Twain developed at least fifty-seven different types of scrapbooks and sold them. Mark Twain House

the paper cut-out figures on her pages in actual fabric swatches. The wonderful thing about looking at an ancestral scrapbook is that it offers you a glimpse into the world in which your ancestor lived. The small details that can enliven a family genealogy are visible in an old scrapbook.

Today, it's a rare scrapbook that doesn't include photographs. Although earlier generations of scrapbookers began using images in their albums in the mid-nineteenth century, it wasn't until the Kodak camera became available in the 1880s that photographs started to appear along with scrap in most albums. (Photograph albums are not considered a type of scrapbook because they only contain images.) Interest in scrapbooks waned in the mid-twentieth century

and their format remained unchanged for several decades.

When family history experienced a resurgence of interest in the 1970s due to Alex Haley's *Roots*, scrapbooks once again became a popular hobby. Scrapbookers began using magnetic photo albums with self-adhesive pages and plastic cover sheets. At an international genealogy conference in Salt Lake City in 1980, several individuals exhibited their family scrapbooks. This created a demand for new products, magazines, and preservation information about scrapbooking, thus sparking today's billion-dollar industry. Now it's easier than ever to create a scrapbook with software that allows you to create page layouts and albums on your computer and post them online.

FINDING ANCESTRAL SCRAPBOOKS

Just because you don't own a scrapbook created by an ancestor doesn't mean one doesn't exist. Since scrapbooking was a common pursuit, you are destined to find at least one created by a direct or distant relative. Scrapbook albums are not difficult to locate and may fall into any of the categories listed above: common-place books, friendship albums, extra-illustrated books, or scrapbooks. In fact, most archives and libraries have them in family manuscript collections. You might get lucky and locate an album for your family by using the same techniques described in future chapters to find other types of family material. Each one of these research methods is explained in the skill-building exercises in future chapters in this book:

• Contact all your relatives and see if they know of any scrapbooks created by your ancestors.

• Search online auction sites such as eBay.com for family memorabilia, including scrapbooks.

• See if the local or state historical society has material on your family, including scrapbooks. Contact them directly. See the Appendix for a list of state historical societies.

INTERPRETING ANCESTRAL ALBUMS

While the types of albums our forefathers and mothers kept don't necessarily resemble the ones you create today, they still tell a story if you know what to look for. Interpreting each of the items you locate by using this book is a vital part of understanding your family history and incorporating it into a scrapbook.

At first glance these scrapbooks might seem both confusing and interesting because of their sometimes-odd combinations of materials. If you're lucky, the person who created these albums wrote her name in the book. If she didn't, then you are probably wondering what significance these items have for your family history. Think of them as a puzzle waiting to be put together. Each page contains pieces of the daily life and interests of a family member: someone you don't know very well outside of a name, date, and a few details. The type of scrapbook and what it contains can tell a story if you know what to look for.

Your first step in interpreting an ancestral scrapbook is to examine the inside front cover to see if there is a signature that identifies the maker. Next, look for a title page. Some individuals chose themes for their books, titled them, and sometimes wrote short introductions. Carefully turn the pages and look over each one. Go through the album completely to get a sense of what the creator collected for its pages and if the type of material changed as time passed.

• **_Was the album created by one person or added to later by another individual?_** Just because it is a single scrapbook doesn't mean the original creator didn't let someone else add to it later. For instance, a mother might have started the book when she was a young woman, and then taken it out of storage to let her children make additions.

• Who created it? If you don't know the compiler's name, can you tell if it was a male or female, adult or child? You'll be surprised by the similarities between what children collect today and what they did a hundred years ago. Nineteenth-century boys didn't accumulate pictures of girls' toys any more than they do today.

• What type of scrap is on the page? You can date a scrapbook by using city directories to find dates of operation for a business or by researching product labels that may be included. If you have a friendship album like the one created by Hellen Marion Adams, you'll be able to research each of the people who left tokens in the book and discover new family relationships.

• Is there a theme? Is the album a collection of family material, random scraps artistically arranged, or did it have a particular purpose? For instance, one woman created a wedding scrapbook with memorabilia from her bridal showers including a list and description of gifts, many of which are still in the family today. Other scrapbooks may be strictly ornamental.

Heritage Album Idea:
Recreate the look of an ancestral scrapbook with the techniques used in historical albums. See Chapter 7 for more details.

CARING FOR ANCESTRAL ALBUMS

What can you do to preserve the ancestral scrapbooks that you find or own? A lot depends on the materials used to create them. Unless they were made before 1865, approximately the year paper began to be made from wood pulp, then the pages are going to be extremely brittle and yellowed due to the acid and lignin contained in the paper. Lignin is the substance that turns newspaper yellow. Adhesives used to paste items on the page can deteriorate so that pieces are falling out of the album. Don't despair. There are steps you can take to keep these books around for several more generations. The most expensive solution is to consult a paper conservator. A free list of conservators in your area is available from the American Institute for Conservation of Historic and Artistic Works <aic.stanford.edu>. A conservator can stabilize the damage and stop the deterioration. A less expensive solution is to purchase acid- and lignin-free papers and boxes from suppliers and store the scrapbooks with pages interleaved with acid- and lignin-free papers.

Here are a few tips to save your ancestral scrapbooks:

Handle Them Carefully

The fragility of the paper and the scraps means that you can unintentionally break off pieces of the album page. Loose fragments can also float out of the album, so slowly turn the pages when looking at them.

Store in a Stable Environment

Changes in temperature and humidity can affect the life of an album. The rate of deterioration directly relates to heat and moisture. Store your scrapbooks in a windowless closet in special storage containers. (See Chapter 9 for additional information.)

Long-Term Storage

Use materials that will help prolong the life of your scrapbook, especially those tested for use with scrapbooks. It also helps to wrap albums in acid- and lignin-free paper so that loose pieces aren't lost before placing them in the acid- and lignin-free boxes with reinforced corners.

The Next Step

Many scrapbook hobbyists are also busy trying to preserve family memorabilia including scrapbooks created by their ancestors. If you want to create your own scrapbook commemorating your family, you'll need a variety of simple genealogical research skills to find and tell the story of your family as well as different types of documents to bring them back to life. By the end of this book, you'll be able to tell the story of the items as well as bring the members of your family tree back to life through images and information. Family history is a fascinating pursuit, so let's get started.

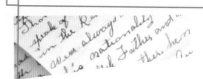

RESOURCES

Books

A Victorian Scrapbook by Cynthia Hart and John Grossman (Workman Publishing, 1989)

On Women and Friendship: A Collection of Victorian Keepsakes and Traditions (Stewart, Tabori and Chang, 1993)

Web Sites

Preservation of Scrapbooks and Albums by the Library of Congress ←lcweb.loc.gov/ preserv/care/scrapbk.html → online leaflet covers collection policies, environment, physical storage and shelving, handling, treatment and reformatting, and sources of supplies.

Scrapbook History

←www.tulane.edu/~wclib/ scrapbooks.html→ View a variety of scrapbooks online, look at a timeline, and read an extensive bibliography courtesy of Tulane University.

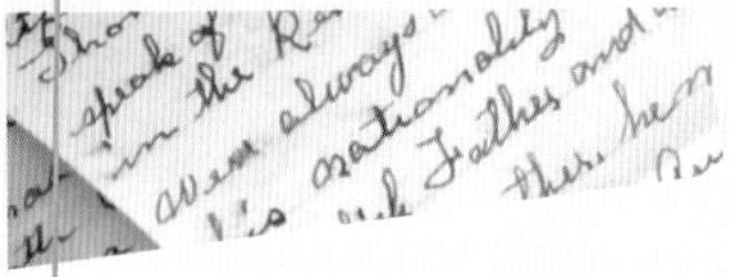

TIMELINE OF SCRAPBOOKING HISTORY

1520   1540   1560   1580   1600   1620   1640   1660   1680   1700   1720   1740   1760

1598

A gathering
of "words and
approved phrases
...to make use as it
were a common
place booke [sic]."

1706

Philosopher John
Locke publishes
his *New Method
of Making Common-
place Books.*

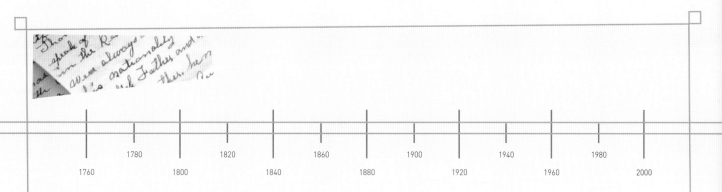

1760   1780   1800   1820   1840   1860   1880   1900   1920   1940   1960   1980   2000

1769
William Granger introduces a book that includes extra blank pages for collecting scrap.

1800s
Young women keep friendship albums of scrap and memorabilia.

1825
A magazine, *The Scrapbook*, begins publication with articles on the hobby.

1837
Godefroye Englemann invents chromolithography, a process of lithograph in color from a series of plates. This invention makes it possible to produce colorful scrap for inclusion in albums.

1860s
Mass production of advertising cards for companies and products.

1867
John Jerrard of London calls himself a dealer in photographs and scrap prints of every description for albums and scrapbooks.

1872
Mark Twain markets his self-pasting scrapbook.

1880
E.W. Gurley publishes *Scrapbooks and How to Make Them*.

1888
George Eastman sells cameras for amateurs with the slogan, "You push the button, we do the rest."

1900
Major publishers begin marketing themed scrapbooks for children and adults.

1945
Books Across the Sea sponsors a contest for children's scrapbooks with cash prizes.

1980
The Christensens display their scrapbooks at the World Conference on Genealogy in Salt Lake City.

1996
Memory Makers magazine begins publication.

CHAPTER ONE

GETTING STARTED

Genealogy: Tracing your family history
by researching each ancestor—male and female.

S o, you are interested in finding out who sits on the branches of your family tree because a relative left you a box of family material. Or perhaps you enjoy creating scrapbook pages of your living family and now want to turn to heritage albums. Genealogy is a fascinating hobby, one that is full of adventure and details. Even if you don't uncover any famous or infamous ancestors and you end up hitting what genealogists call a "brick wall," or dead end, you can still create a piece of family memorabilia based on a single person or a whole branch of the family. Ultimately, you determine what makes this creation a special keepsake and who to feature in it. Don't despair if you lack materials in your own collection; you'll find new photographs and stories as you contact family and research ancestors. What materials you locate depends on where you look, so follow these steps to explore the possibilities.

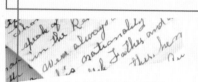

HOME SOURCES AND MORE

- Documents
- Photographs
- Memorabilia
- Artifacts
- Ancestral scrapbooks

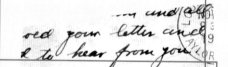

Why should you research your family tree? While every individual has a personal reason for learning more about family history, here are some of the top ones:

- Curiosity about family stories

- Trying to find a connection to royalty or a famous person

- Reconnecting with "lost" family members

- Discovering family medical history

- Interested in joining a lineage society such the Daughters of the American Revolution.

START WITH WHAT YOU KNOW

If you want to create a family history scrapbook or other art work, you'll need a place to start. Begin by thinking about what you know about your family. Write down the details using a pedigree chart (see page 26) that outlines family information. You'll be amazed at the knowledge you've picked up over the years—and by what you don't know. For each person on your "tree," list when and where he was born, married, and died, and his full name, leaving blanks for unknown data. Most people know some of the details and even own a few artifacts, so it is usually possible to name people and dates for at least a few generations. Remember to work backwards one step at a time so that you can see your family in relation to each other. Keep in mind the historical events that influenced your ancestor's decisions. For instance, you might learn that several individuals served in World War I. These facts will help you track down additional material on those relatives.

HOME SOURCES

Research is definitely part of the family history discovery process, but not until you've interviewed relatives and located additional resources in your family. When you start to fill in your tree, you'll probably remember all the documents or clippings you've saved and stored in boxes, Bibles, and safety deposit boxes. Birth certificates, obituaries, passports, and handwritten notes add names and dates to your family history. Keepsakes and artifacts are also important. A simple piece of jewelry can tell the story of a courtship, while postcards and membership cards inform you about family interests and hobbies. Each piece of paper, story, or artifact helps you fill in the blanks on your family tree. Drag out of storage everything you can find, from old wedding gowns to home movies, and re-examine each one for clues. One woman found proof in an old postcard that her family was from Norway and discovered that distant relatives still live there.

Heritage Album Idea:

Ask relatives if they can be quoted, then include copies of their E-mails on acid- and lignin-free paper. You can also use transcripts of parts of the interview, or copied selections from handwritten letters.

INTERVIEW LIVING RELATIVES

Once you've recalled what you can about your family and looked at materials you own, turn to other family members for help. Make note of all the relatives who might be able to assist you in your search for family data, and then contact each one with a list of questions in hand. Preparing beforehand helps keep the interview focused. Don't forget to ask about documents, photographs, and artifacts they might own. While they probably won't want to part with them, most people are proud of what they have and will usually let you copy or photograph the material. Contact your relatives NOW so you don't lose their stories. Too many people procrastinate until it is too late and family stories have died with a relative. If someone doesn't want to talk about the family, be patient, it might take time to convince them of your good intentions. Bring along any heritage photographs in your possession, something for taking notes (a tape recorder is helpful), and your pedigree chart. Keep separate notes for each individual you talk with or write to. The photographs you bring with you help jog their memories and may uncover a few new identifications.

It's so easy to get carried away when researching ancestors that you forget to keep good notes and jump ahead, creating relationships based on assumptions rather than facts. Take time to keep track of all your sources. Try to focus on one person at a time before moving on so you don't end up climbing someone else's family tree. In families where there are relatives with the same name, staying focused will avoid confusion. Check the facts of a story by locating documents or other material to verify what you know or have learned. Once you have the basics, it's time to try to locate new material.

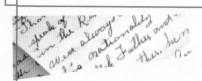

THE ORAL HISTORY INTERVIEW

Oral history is gathering information and stories from people by interviewing them.

Tools:

Tape recorder, video recorder, paper and pencil, copies of old photographs and documents, and a family tree chart.

Questions:

- Where were you born?
- What were your parents' names?
- Where have you lived?
- What was your occupation?
- Do you have any family documents, photographs, memorabilia, or artifacts?

These are just a few of the questions you might want to ask a relative. A guide to oral history interviewing appears on the American Memory section of the Library of Congress Web site ←www.cms.ccsd.k12.co.us/ ss/SONY/orbeta/orlguide.htm→. Although it is intended for children, anyone can learn the basics from the site's lessons. Additional interview advice appears in Emily Anne Croom's *Unpuzzling Your Past* 4th edition (Betterway Books, 2001) and Katherine Scott Sturdevant's *Bringing Your Family History to Life Through Social History* (Betterway Books, 2000).

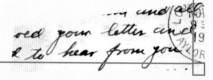

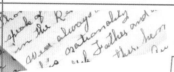

SKILL-BUILDING: USING A SIMPLE PEDIGREE CHART

Believe it or not, the word pedigree refers to a crane's foot, which resembles the chart used by genealogists to trace their lineage. A blank, standard pedigree chart appears in the appendix or you can download one for free at ←www.familytree magazine.com→. See Chapter 6 for an explanation of other ways to chart your research. You can also use a genealogical software package for your family tree. Additional information on software options appear in Chapter 10.

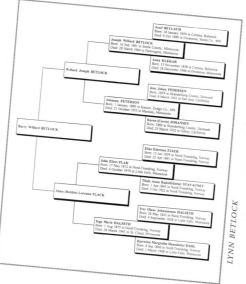

LYNN BETLOCK

FAMILY HISTORY TOOLS

- Charts
- Pencils
- Notebook
- Camera
- Change for making copies

STAYING ORGANIZED

- Work backwards, one person in a family at a time.
- Consult home sources.
- Verify your sources by referencing original documents.
- Use a pedigree chart to see at a glance what you know and still need.
- Set a goal.

ORGANIZE AS YOU GO

Rather than wait until you have heaps of paper, photographs, and information, start organizing your family history material as you go. This will save you time later on and make it easier for you to find items to include in your album. As you accumulate material you can:

• Place them in acid- and lignin-free folders arranged by surname. Put the folders in a box that you can carry with you on visits.

Heritage Album Tip:
It's never too early to start gathering layout ideas by looking at books on heritage albums, magazine articles, and even historical pieces. Keep copies of those layout ideas in a folder for future reference.

• Use photo corners to temporarily attach items to plain acid- and lignin-free paper to make an album you can carry around to relatives. Don't forget to include captions that mention where you found the item.

These tips will enable you to bring only what you need to a relative's house when you interview them about their family. Don't forget to practice your scrapbooking techniques with your new photographs in preparation for working with older materials. See Chapter 8 for other organizing tips.

See the list of suppliers in the Appendix for materials to preserve your ancestral albums.

Look for religious records, cemetery markers, and vital records. Collection of the author.

RESEARCH

There comes a time in every genealogy project when you want to know more than relatives and home sources can tell you. Resources such as census records, cemetery records, and vital records create a context for images, artifacts, and family information. See below for an explanation of each of these resources. Locate them by using libraries and archives or turn to the largest library in the world—the Internet.

Online, you can search databases, locate lost family photographs, and even reconnect with cousins. It only takes a few moments on the Web to realize that there are an overwhelming number of Web sites containing genealogical material—everything from family sites to subscription databases. Start by exploring the options. Most Web sites contain a mixture of research help and subscription services. Many sites feature free e-newsletters to keep users up-to-date with new offerings. Before you spend a cent on family history research, try a variety of sites, see what's offered for free, then pick a

subscription based on your research needs. To make the best use of the Web, keep a list of sites used and results so that you don't duplicate your efforts. It's so easy to lose track of your path when clicking through the Web. Using the Internet is a real time-saver, but remember to double-check all the information to be sure it is correct by locating documents such as those listed below.

CHECKLIST OF BASIC SOURCES

Census Records: Every ten years since 1790, the United States government has taken a population census. The amount of information collected varies from census to census. Unfortunately only small portions of the 1890 Federal Census still exist due to a fire. Federal census records are available at branches of the National Archives or at large public, academic or special genealogical libraries. A list of U.S. National Archives and Records Administration locations is online at <www.archives.gov>. Depending on

where you live, there may also be state census records or Colonial census material. There is a lot to learn about census records beyond the basics and Kathleen W. Hinckley fills you in on the details in *Your Guide to the Federal Census: For Genealogists, Researchers, and Family Historians* (Betterway Books, 2002).

Cemetery Records: If you can't locate a death record, you might be able to find the data you seek on a gravestone. Once again, it depends on where you live, if the records still exist, and if you can find the gravestone. Try contacting cemeteries in the area your ancestor lived first to see if records exist, and don't forget to search online databases such as <www.rootsweb.com> for transcriptions.

Religious Records: Congregations like to keep track of their members from birth to death, so it is always a good

Marriage record of J.H. Betlock and Hannah Petersen

LYNN BETLOCK

VERIFYING YOUR SOURCES

• Locate other documents that contain similar information such as birth dates.

• Double-check everything you find on the Internet or in print by locating original documents and by finding as many sources of data as you can for each person.

idea to try to locate these records for your ancestors. They may help you overcome brick walls in your research or discover a few surprises. For instance, you might discover your ancestors were a very different denomination from your own. Records are either kept with the religious congregation, the diocese or are sometimes donated to historical societies and other special collection libraries.

Military Records: Is there a rumor in your family of a Revolutionary War or Civil War ancestor? If so, then you need to track down the military papers for that individual in a local or state archives, or even the National Archives in Washington, DC. You might discover physical characteristics, a medical chart of war injuries, or a pension file full of letters written by neighbors and family in support of the applicant's pension. There are sources of information for military conflicts from the colonial period through the present. (See Chapter 10 for more details.)

Vital Records: The availability of birth, marriage, and death records depends on the state in which your ancestors lived. In some areas civil registration for this information didn't occur until the early twentieth century. A few states have access to older records online. These documents (when complete) generally provide names, dates, and parents' names, but there is some variety. Many records from Colonial times have been published. For additional material on using vital records, consult *The Source* edited by Loretto Dennis Szucs (Ancestry, 1997).

WORKING FROM HOME

Family history research used to mean visiting courthouses, reading dusty records in town halls, and writing endless correspondence. It still does much of the time, but now there are multiple ways to find information without leaving your computer. You still have to double-check and verify any information found online, but the convenience of using the Internet 24/7 is pretty handy.

ACCESS CARD CATALOGS AND RESEARCH HELPS

Don't know where to look for information on your ancestral hometown? Start by searching an online card catalog for a historical society, archive, or public library in that area. You can even search the nation's largest library, the Library of Congress <www.loc.gov>, and find books, documents, and photographs all with a few key strokes. You can also find research manuals to help you locate material on your family.

FIND ANCESTORS ONLINE

The breadth and wealth of family information available online is astounding. You never know what you are going to find, so start with some general sites to help you find your way around and explore your roots.

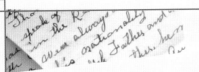

WEB SITES TO GET STARTED

Cyndi's List

←www.cyndislist.com→ is similar to a card catalog arranged by subject with sublistings in each category.

Family Tree Magazine

←www.familytreemagazine.com→ features previews of articles from the print magazine, online columns, and a search engine for finding information by surname, keyword, living people, or resources.

FamilySearch

←www.familysearch.org→ is the vast database of the Church of Jesus Christ of Latter-day Saints. Search for ancestors all over the world in the International Genealogical Index match and match results with other researchers on Ancestral File.

RootsWeb

←www.rootsweb.com→ has databases, message boards, and educational material for the beginning genealogist.

Ancestry.com

←www.ancestry.com→ of MyFamily.com maintains an archive of its free, daily e-newsletter and offers family tree software and surname message boards. But the real strength of this site lies in its searchable subscription databases, census records, maps, and genealogical periodical index. It also features a message board.

Genealogy.com

←www.genealogy.com→ entices users with MyGenealogy.com, a feature that enables you to save your genealogical searches and trees. You can access an online data library that consists of several separate subscriptions from digitized pages, research contributed by users, census records, and databases. You may also post queries on the message boards.

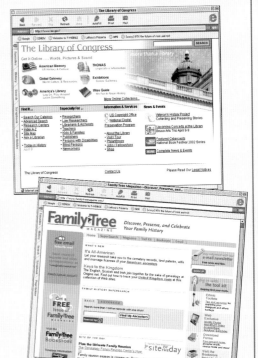

Library of Congress Home Page
<www.loc.gov>
Family Tree Magazine Home Page
<www.familytreemagazine.com>

CONNECTING TO COUSINS ONLINE

Before computers, family historians placed queries—questions about their ancestors—in print periodicals. A few daring souls even sent letters to local newspapers hoping a kind editor would publish the inquiries. Some papers such as the *Boston Transcript* and the *Hartford Courant* devoted space to special genealogical columns. Today, the Internet has made it easier than ever to form alliances with genealogists researching the same ancestors as you.

The Web is now the place to post queries or answers to genealogical puzzles. The format is very similar to the newspaper and periodical columns. You can share information and make amazing discoveries simply by placing a query online. While it hasn't yet happened to me, friends tell me about finding cousins in all parts of the country. They have also located additional family photographs for their collections and uncovered research clues. With these new family Web contacts, it is possible to form new friendships and share the genealogical workload. Of course, you

can still use newspaper or magazine columns to post your questions. The International Society of Family History Writers and Editors Web site <www.rootsweb.com/~cgc/cgc3.htm> contains a link to these print columns on its "News Stand" page at <www.siteone.com/clubs/mgs/newsstand.htm>.

It is the immediacy of placing a query online that attracts many family historians. With so many message boards and forums to choose from, you need to know how to increase your odds of making a successful connection.

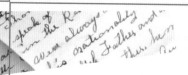

SKILL BUILDING: WRITING A SAMPLE QUERY

If you want to see some sample queries, look at the examples on the RootsWeb site, ←www.rootsweb. com/~mistclai/queries/sample queries.html→, which also includes some humorous examples of what not to do. Elizabeth Kerstens offers advice in her online article "Writing Effective Electronic Queries" at ←www.ancestry.com/library/view/ columns/extra/3976.asp→. You can also follow the guidelines offered by the National Genealogical Society in an article titled "Good Queries are Clear—Specific—Simple—Concise" at ←www.ngsgenealogy.org/news queriesgood.htm→. In general, the basic guidelines for queries are:

• **Keep it short**
Most individuals do not want to read long queries. For instance, RootsWeb has specific guidelines to follow regarding content.

• **Make it easy to understand and read**
Focus your query and stay on the topic. Don't include extraneous information not related to the question.

• **Check your grammar and spelling**
Always double-check these two items. After all, you are presenting your data in a public forum. Give your requests a professional look with correct spelling and grammar.

• **Include your contact information**
You generally need to provide an e-mail contact for responses. If you are not comfortable with your primary e-mail address appearing in such a public forum, consider signing up for a free e-mail account through a provider such as Yahoo!, Hotmail or *Family Tree Magazine's* Web site.

• **Follow the rules**
It's a good idea to read the frequently asked questions (FAQs) or guidelines for each message board before proceeding. Rootsweb, for instance, requires certain formatting so that your message can appear online. There are restrictions on all lists. Never include any type of advertising material or anything that could be construed as a copyright violation. Remember to keep your message appropriate to the board you are on and you'll be all right.

SEARCH FIRST

Before posting your own research problem, find out what already exists. There may be hundreds of postings to wade through for a common surname, but most lists allow you to conduct keyword searches. If you aren't sure where to begin, check out the links on <www.cyndislist.com> under "Queries." You'll find sites that post messages on surnames, places, and topics. When visiting such sites, you will note that each query generally appears with its main topic, a link to the person submitting it, and the date it first appeared. Any responses, also known as threads, appear with the original query. Search as many lists as you can. Select topics or surnames related to your query. The GenForum message boards at <www.genealogy.com> allow you to save your searches in an area called "My GenForum," so that you can easily replicate searches. With so many lists to choose from, your chances of finding matches are better on more active lists. You can tell how active a list is by looking at the number of postings it receives daily and the size of its directory. If you find a posting that seems relevant, send a quick private message to the person who submitted the query or add your answer to the thread of messages following the question. If you don't turn up any hits, it is time for you to add your own research question to the board.

POSTING QUERIES

There are several things you need to keep in mind when creating your query. Be specific. While you don't want to tell people your whole family history, you need to include some facts or risk never receiving responses. In general, you want to keep queries short and to the point. State the name and dates of the person you seek and any information you have that helps identify him or her. Then explain why you are posting the query. It might be helpful to list briefly what data you are not interested in receiving. For instance, if you already have a marriage record for the couple, include those details so that you don't receive duplicates.

Again, post your query on a busy site; the larger audience increases your odds of receiving a reply. If you don't find a board that applies to your surname, topic, or locality, ask the board administrator to add a new category.

SIGN UP FOR A MAILING LIST

Another option is subscribing to a surname mailing list that will send you e-mail updates. Just beware that if you have a common surname, you could receive an abundance of mail. If you don't have a common surname, subscribing to a list may work out fine. Keep in mind that you'll probably want to sign up for several lists to cover all the surnames you're researching, as well as places where your ancestors lived. If the mail becomes overwhelming, you can always remove yourself from the list. Adding your name to a mailing list is certainly worth a try.

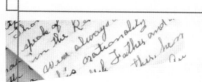

BASIC TYPES OF MESSAGE BOARDS

Surname
Post queries on a particular relative. For questions regarding your female relatives, list them on boards with both their married and maiden names.

Locality
If you know your ancestor came from a particular area or spent a short amount of time there, you might want to ask for advice regarding resources. You can also duplicate your surname query on a locality forum.

Topic
Want to share information on searching for relatives in prison records? Then post your query on a topical board. There are a wide variety of boards that cover subjects varying from adoptions to photographs.

- **NewEnglandAncestors.org**
  ←www.newenglandancestors.org/forum/vsforum.asp→ Search and post messages in this site's discussion forums based on surname, locality, or topic. Messages can be viewed in different formats. E-mail notification of new postings is available. These forums are free to the public.

- **Ancestry.com**
  ←boards.ancestry.com→ Look through the message boards organized by surname, locality, and topic. For instance, one topic board focuses on genealogical software. This site has a FAQ page to help users.

- **Cyndi's List**
  ←www.cyndislist.com→ This is a good general starting place for individuals looking for a message board that is locality-specific or for help formatting a request.

- **National Genealogical Society**
  ←www.ngsgenealogy.org/news-queries.htm→ Queries appear on this Web site for six months. Use the link to "How to Write a Good Query" prior to submitting.

- **GenForum at Genealogy.com**
  ←www.GenForum.genealogy.com→ Try searching or posting messages on one or more of the boards relating to surnames, topics, or localities. You can narrow your search by selecting a feature that allows you to look at just new postings, those from the current day, the last seven days, or all messages. You can also look for specific keywords in all the messages or those for just the message board you are in. Messages are archived and nothing is deleted.

- **RootsWeb**
  ←www.rootsweb.com→ Adding your query to the Rootsweb Surname List (RSL) is easy as long as you follow the formatting suggestions, which are posted at ←helpdesk.rootsweb.com/help/rsl6.html#Submit→. There are only five requirements, including submitting the name in upper and lowercase letters and including your contact information.

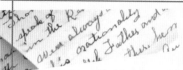

HERALDRY: TRUTH AND MYTH

The truth is hard to accept; there are no family crests or coats of arms. Yet the myth of a family crest is perpetuated by companies selling them to individuals. Heraldry or coats of arms were developed in the Middle Ages as a way to identify soldiers on the battlefield. A woman could use her father's heraldic coat of arms, and when she married that became part of her husband's shield design.

In order to use a coat of arms, you need to prove that you are a direct male and first-born descendant of the person to whom it originally belonged. If you can trace your ancestry back to the person who received the original crest, feel free to use it for personal use; if not, don't perpetuate the myth.

It is possible to create your own coat of arms. Two organizations in the United States recognize new coats of arms: the New England Historic

Coats of arms were issued to individuals. New England Historic Genealogical Society.

Genealogical Society, 101 Newbury St., Boston, MA 02116; and the American College of Heraldry in Maryland ←www.americancollegeofheraldry.org/acheraldry.html→ P.O. Box 710, Cottondale, AL 35453. Consult Patricia Lovett's *Calligraphy & Illumination: A History & Practical Guide* (Harry Abrams, 2000) for step-by-step instructions on creating your own coat of arms and Sharon DeBartolo Carmack's article "Unzipping Your Coat of Arms" in *Family Tree Magazine* (August 2000).

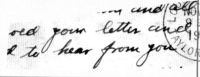

resources that might help you.

Since your goal is to compile an attractive visual history of your family, there are plenty of ways to express it. Your final product will be a combination of genealogical data, pictures, and creativity. With all the materials on the market, you can use just about anything, and let your imagination run wild.

As an intergenerational hobby, family history brings relatives of all ages closer together in their search for a mutual past. Now that you know the first steps see what else you can create.

TRANSCRIBING DATES

As you collect information on ancestors, you are apt to see dates that look confusing, such as 1723/24 or other variations. Therefore, it's important to transcribe the date from a document exactly how it appears rather than trying to convert it into a standard calendar format. Why? Well, to us, the second month of the year is February, but that wasn't necessarily true for our ancestors. For instance, Quakers considered April the second month in their year. Americans usually write out a date as month/day/year while Europeans use day/month/year. When writing dates for family history, it helps to write out the month, such as 12 November 2002, to avoid any confusion.

Resources
• *The Ancestry Family Historian's Address Book: A Comprehensive List of Addresses of Local, State, & Federal Agencies & Institutions* by Juliana Szucs Smith (Compiler) (Ancestry, 1998)

• *Ancestry's Red Book: American State, County and Town Resources* edited by Alice Eichholz (Editor), William Dollarhide (Ancestry, 1997)

• *The Family Tree Guidebook* by the Editors of *Family Tree Magazine* (Betterway Books, 2002)

WHAT'S NEXT?

There are plenty of people making online family research connections. Just be cautious. Before you send off copies of all your research to someone you don't really know, establish the relationship to your family tree. If you receive that person's research files, be sure to check sources. As every good researcher knows, it's important to verify information from fellow researchers before you decide to work with them on a project. You want to make sure their research standards are the same as yours.

Posting a query is a gamble, but I love the Web for its ability to connect individuals around the world. You might find that someone living in the United States or even a distant relative overseas has the information you need. You can also use online lists to find out about

TIMELINE OF GENEALOGICAL MILESTONES

1450	1550	1650	1750	1850	1950
1400	1500	1600	1700	1800	1900	2000

Pre-1600
Tax records, court documents, and land transactions are primary tools for tracing family history.

1538
English Parish records begin being recorded.

1607
Jamestown becomes the first English settlement in what will become the United States.

1620
The Puritans land at Plymouth (Massachusetts).

1790
The first U.S. federal census is taken, listing heads of families.

1837
Civil registration of birth, marriage, and death records required in Great Britain.

1845
The New England Historic Genealogical Society is the first genealogical society in the United States.

1850
The U.S. federal census is taken, listing all members of a household.

1922
April 13—Most Irish records are destroyed in a fire in Dublin.

1954
Denmark organizes the International Confederation of Genealogy and Heraldry.

1984
Family Tree Maker is first offered as a genealogical software package.

CHAPTER TWO

WHAT DID YOUR ANCESTOR LOOK LIKE?

T here is a rumor among your relatives that the family nose (which you unfortunately inherited) descends from Great-great-great-uncle Harry. You'd love to find a picture to see if he's really responsible for this facial feature, but don't know where to look. Family images can be found in many different places. Photographic portraits immediately come to mind, but there are many other media to consider.

When Louis Daguerre invented the daguerreotype, the first type of photographic image, in 1839, he was just one of many individuals looking for a new way to capture a realistic likeness of people and places. For centuries, professional and amateur artists had employed a variety of techniques from paintings to engravings to memorialize a person. Americans loved to have their likenesses captured by itinerant artists, who frequently painted their subjects' heads on top of a pre-painted portrait. Sitting for a silhouette was a popular form of entertainment in the eighteenth century. You can also uncover written accounts of what an ancestor looked like. In fact, Colonial Americans used a standard descriptive vocabulary when posting advertisements in local newspapers to enable citizens to spot and apprehend criminals, as well as runaway slaves and servants.

Whether you're looking for the genetic origins of family traits or to fill in the blanks in an illustrated family tree or a scrapbook, a little detective work can often turn up visual evidence.

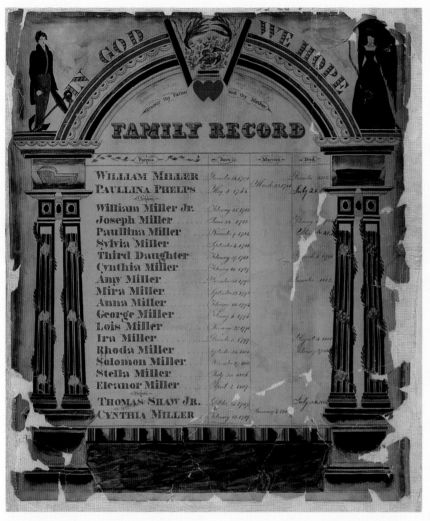

Family Record for William Miller and Paulina Phelps. New England Historic Genealogical Society

Family records: Before the dawn of photography, artistically inclined family members created illustrated family records with genealogical information that sometimes included watercolor portraits or pen-and-ink drawings.

Paintings: In the mid-fourteenth century, Emperor Charles IV of Prague commissioned a genealogical series of portraits of sixty ancestors and relatives. Unfortunately for royal genealogists, many of the portraits are not of real people but rather mythological figures—so Charles' family portrait album looked a little different than yours. Commissioned portraits were for the wealthy or artists and their families, but there are a few rare collections of ancestral portraits passed from parents to children. Most painted portraits end up in museums or are simply lost.

Photographs: The first photograph, the daguerreotype, was taken in 1839. It became an inexpensive way to obtain a portrait from a professional photographer. When George Eastman introduced candid photography for amateurs in 1888, thousands of people began taking pictures as a hobby.

Portrait miniatures: Prominent families commissioned artists to paint miniature portraits, usually on enamel or ivory, that could be worn as a brooch or locket. Meant for private viewing, some were as small as one and one-quarter inches framed. These miniatures originated with the English monarchy in the sixteenth century; Queen Elizabeth I had a whole collection. Miniatures often depicted such milestones as childhood, marriage, immigration, and death. Painter John Singleton Copley introduced the art form to America in the eighteenth century.

Printed reproductions: Engravings and lithographs are two types of printed reproductions that appeared before photography. These could be copies of existing paintings or prints of original portraits. Engravings are cut into a plate, usually steel or wood, while lithographs are printed from ink or crayon applied to a stone surface. These types of images appeared in books, were sold as single sheets, and eventually appeared in newspapers. Today you can use printed reference guides and online resources to locate printed reproductions.

Silhouettes: These black-paper shadow portraits, profiles, or shades appeared in the mid-eighteenth century. Individuals would sit before a lamp casting a shadow on a wall. The shadow was traced, and the resulting design was cut from a single sheet of paper. The silhouettes were commonly framed with the person's name written beneath the likeness. In the late eighteenth century, silhouettes became quite popular because of the belief that you could tell a person's character from the shape of the head.

Written descriptions: In eighteenth-century America, newspapers and posters ("broadsides") helped inform residents of happenings in their area and the world. The typical newspaper was just four pages long, with the back page dedicated to advertisements, some of a personal nature.

You might find a description of your ancestor in a newspaper or broadside. For instance, relatives of one Benjamin Cleveland might be dismayed to discover a Revolutionary War deserter in their family but delighted to know that in 1776 he was "19 years old, 5 feet 4 inches high, light complexion, red hair, light eyes, born in Newport" and was a mariner. Such printed descriptions served as sort of the verbal equivalent of a police sketch.

Portrait of Charles Ewer (1796-1853). New England Historic Genealogical Society.

UNRAVELING PHOTOGRAPHIC MYSTERIES

Most of us have mysterious old photographs in our own collections. Maybe some photos have a first name but not a date, or there's partial information passed on through family lore. But most such images haunt us with their lack of identifying information. Some techniques for identifying photographs are described below. Many of these methods can also help you date a painted portrait or engraving.

SIMPLE PHOTOGRAPHIC IDENTIFICATION

Here are a few simple steps to get you started solving your photographic mysteries.

Ask Questions
The first step in any investigation is to ask questions. Your research will try to determine the answers. First, consider if there are any relatives who might be able to supply additional material or stories related to the photo. Try to record their recollections in case you need to refer to them again later, by transcribing their memories or by using a tape or video recorder. Make sure you keep track of full contact information for anyone you interview. Show them the photograph several times during the identification process in case some new information jogs their memory.

Here Are Some Sample Questions:
- What do you know about the image?

- Who was its previous owner?

- Is it part of a larger collection?

- Are there any stories associated with it?

- Do you know why it was taken?

- Do you know when it was taken?

- Do you know any of the people in the picture?

- Did a family member supply the identification?

Keep Track of Your Research
In order to draw conclusions based on your inquiries, document your research using a worksheet. This will also help you develop a research plan. You'll want to include such basic information as the owner's name, contact information, condition of the image, size, if it is an original or copy, and any other data you accumulate. You'll be able to include some of these details in a caption about the image in your scrapbook.

Get Ready to Research
Since you'll be showing your picture to relatives and taking it with you to libraries, you should make either a same-size photocopy of both sides of the photograph or a copy photograph so that you aren't carrying an irreplaceable original. Make multiple copies so you can send them to relatives who may have similar photographs in their collections. Get the best possible copy your budget allows so the details remain visible.

What Type of Photograph Is It?

Determining the type of photograph can help you decide if the image is of your fourth-great-grandmother or your great-grandmother. Here is a brief outline of the types of images prevalent in the nineteenth century and early twentieth century.

(RIGHT)
Unidentified daguerreotype, c. 1855. Collection of the author.

(FAR RIGHT)
Unidentified ambrotype, c. 1860. Collection of the author.

- **Daguerreotype (1839-1860s):** Metal photograph with a reflective surface, sometimes found in a case. They must be held at an angle to be seen.

- **Ambrotype (invented 1854):** Negative image on glass that appears as a positive because of its dark backing material. They were usually placed in a case because of their fragility.

- **Ferreotype or tintype (invented 1856):** These dark metal images are on thin sheets of iron. Photographers sold them in cases, with paper mats, or alone.

Unidentified tintype. Collection of the author.

- **Paper Print (1859 to the present):** Images on paper were available in a variety of sizes and colors ranging from brown to a purple tinge. Candid images became widespread when George Eastman introduced the Kodak camera in the 1880s.

List the photo's physical characteristics on your worksheet. Is it on metal? Does it look like a mirror? Is it a paper print or on glass? What is its exact size? By answering these questions, you're eliminating possibilities. For example, the earliest type of photographic image, the daguerreotype, was on a shiny metal surface. It actually needs to be held at a particular angle in order to see the image. It was used for a relatively brief, twenty-year period. But another type of metal image, the tintype, was introduced in 1856 and

Unidentified paper prints; The blue one is a cyanotype first introduced in 1880. Collection of the author.

remained popular until the early twentieth century. Creating a checklist of characteristics will help you narrow your choices.

Who Is the Photographer?

The presence of a photographer's name, also known as an imprint, can be a shortcut to deciding on a time frame. In the nineteenth and early twentieth centuries, photographers could order cards preprinted with their name and address on either the front or back. They would then mount photographs on the cards. The resulting combination provided a sturdy support for the image and advertising for the photographer. You can discover a photography studio's dates of operation by searching city directories (found in libraries) of the area in which the photographers operated, contacting the local historical society, or consulting a published directory of photographers for that locale.

What Are They Wearing?

One of the most important details in the dating process involves clothing. In many cases, determining the type of photographic process and a photographer's dates of operation will still leave you with too broad a time frame for genealogical identification. Clothing elements become key to narrowing down the date. In general, fashion changes are most notable in the accessories of a woman's costume such as hats, hairstyle, and jewelry. Costume encyclopedias and fashion magazines (check your local public or academic library for these resources) can help you trace when certain styles of dress were fashionable. For instance, a woman's leg-o-mutton sleeves date an image to the 1890s while another's woman fingerless gloves provides a timeframe of 1840-1850. See the resource box in this chapter for a list of titles.

Stick to a step-by-step process as you try to develop a theory about the photo-

graph; don't skip ahead to a wrong conclusion. By making a quick assumption based on just one feature, such as the dress, it becomes easy to misunderstand the photograph and assign a wrong date.

Where Are They Standing?

Are there any other clues in the image? In outdoor scenes you can identify a season or establish a list of features. A sign in an image can provide information about a business; city directories can then help you pinpoint a date. Examine each section of the photograph for details. Did the photographer use props? While you probably

can't determine a date based solely on the photographic elements, it can help you create a relationship between other photographs in your collection. Photographers generally used similar props in their images. By grouping photographs together that have similar internal details you may discover that you have a number of images taken by the same photographer around the same time. Combining that with other information may lead you to conclude that these individuals form a family group.

(TOP) The photographer's name and address on this photograph as well as clothing clues can help pinpoint a date. Collection of the author.

(BOTTOM) Sometimes where your ancestors are standing can provide you with additional evidence. Collection of the author.

Resources

- *Dressed for the Photographer: Ordinary Americans and Fashion 1840-1900* by Joan Severa (Kent State University Press, 1995)

- *Textiles for Clothing of the Early Republic, 1800-1850* by Lynne Zacek Bassett (Q Graphics, 2001)

- *Textiles for Early Victorian Clothing, 1850-1880* by Susan W. Greene (Q Graphics, 2002)

- *Twentieth Century Fashion* by John Peacock (London: Thames and Hudson, 1993)

- *Victorian Costume for Ladies 1860-1900* by Linda Setnik (Schiffer, 2000)

- *Vintage Hats and Bonnets, 1770-1970* by Susan Langley (Collector Books, 1998)

A PHOTOGRAPHIC MYSTERY

Type of photograph:

The photograph was mounted on a four-by-six-inch card. Consulting a timeline of paper prints helped identify this as a standard size for a type of photograph known as a Cabinet Card. They were introduced in 1866 and were popular into the early 1900s.

Photographer's imprint:

In this case, the photographer, "Bonnell," chose to advertise on the front of the card. By consulting a directory of Western photographers it was determined that a Bonell (listed as "Bonnell") was active in Eau Claire and Chippewa Falls, Wisconsin, from 1875 to 1890.

Clothing details:

The details in the woman's dress and her accessories narrowed that fifteen-year span. The tight sleeves and high puffed shoulder seams were examples of a sleeve style that was in fashion only very briefly, about 1890. By 1893, sleeves were fuller on the upper arm. The rest of her appearance, including her short, frizzed bangs, and a bun at the nape of her neck, agree with that circa-1890 date.

The young man's clothing was a little harder to date since men's fashion changes are not as dramatic. But his basic black sack suit with buttoned vest, white shirt, and silk tie would fit with the late 1880s and early 1890s. By putting all the pieces together, the photo's owner could confidently date the mystery photo at circa 1890.

Unidentified couple, Jackie Hutschmidt

USE YOUR GENEALOGICAL DATA

After completing your photo research, compare what you know to your genealogical research material. It may surprise you to discover you can now place a name with a face. You may also decide that your initial tentative identification was incorrect.

It may take several attempts to identify the most challenging images in your collection. Don't despair. The more people who see your picture and the more you learn, the better your chances of identifying it.

Heritage Album Tip:

Be on the lookout for depictions of the towns your ancestors lived in, examples of occupational dress, places they attended school, maps drawn at the time they lived, and other visuals.

LOCATING IMAGES

The idea of a heritage scrapbook is to photographically document the lives of your ancestors as completely as possible. Don't limit your search to images of people. Include locations, houses, and even cemetery stones. You never know what a photograph can tell you about your family. A caption may say that a child is adopted or an image can include a baby that you're unaware of.

The key to finding pictures, like finding your roots, is methodical research. Think about all the activities your relatives participated in, the places they

Examine your photographs to see if you can guess who was the photographer in your family.

lived, and the people they knew. It really does work and it's a project that will reunite you with long-lost family. Let's look at these ways to build your own family photo collection, even if your ancestors didn't make it easy for you.

List What You Know and What You've Got

Using the family information you already have, make a list of all the people in your family tree who lived from the advent of photography in 1839 to the present. This provides you with an idea of who might be represented in photographs. Highlight the people on this list or on your pedigree charts for whom you already have photographs. Look for any trends. You may discover that you have images of only the maternal side of your family, for example, or of specific branches. Making lists organizes your data and helps provide you with a research plan—a systematic way to track down relatives who may have photographs and to discover other sources.

Start with Home Sources

Think about the photographs you take yourself. They probably focus on particular events and people. Our ancestors also chose to document certain events in their lives; the birth of a new baby was an opportunity to have a new picture taken. Weddings, school, and holidays were also photo opportunities, just as they are today.

Depending on the time frame of the event, families either visited a photographer or took the pictures themselves. Kodak first provided ordinary individuals with a way to document their everyday lives with its "You push the button, we do the rest" mass-produced, portable camera, introduced in 1890.

You may be surprised at the variety

WHAT TO DO IF AN IMAGE IS STILL A MYSTERY

- Show the picture to as many relatives as possible. You don't know when someone will have an identical copy.
- Post it on your Web site or someone else's. There are a number of sites that help to identify photographs or reconnect people with lost family photographs.
- Advertise your family on a message board or query column. While you can't add a photograph to your message or query, you can verbally describe the picture and ask for photographs.
- Re-examine your genealogical data. Are you sure no relatives were living in the area where the photograph was taken?

of images in your relatives' photo collections. Often the last chance to take a picture of someone was after death. This was not unusual and family collections often feature this type of image, known as post-mortem photographs, or a picture of the funeral display. Also, in the twentieth century, it became popular to take photographs of family vacations and compile them in albums.

Network

Just because you don't have many photographs doesn't mean other family members have no photos. Relatives' photo collections may contain "missing" images of your own family. When an estate is divided up, photographs are not usually a significant part of the process. Since wills rarely discuss who inherits family photographs, their fate depends on the mercy of interested relatives.

Go Online

More Web sites and message boards dedicated to photographs are appearing every month. They provide a great opportunity to reconnect with lost pictures and distant relatives or to post your request on a bulletin board for the whole world to see. There are four basic types of Internet-based resources for genealogists interested in photographs:

1. Reunion sites

These sites attempt to reunite photographs found in tag sales and antique shops with their original families. Some charge a fee per image while others consider their mission a public service.

● *Ancient Faces*
<www.ancientfaces.com>
Search and post family photographs.

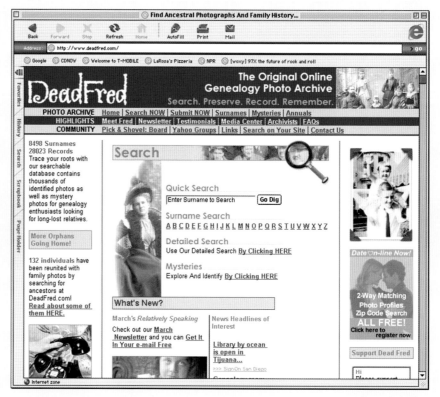

Dead Fred <www.deadfred.com>

● *Ancestral Photos*
<pw1.netcom.com/~cityslic/photos.htm>
Lists photographs found at auctions and in antique stores. Each caption contains a brief description of the items.

● *Dead Fred*
<www.deadfred.com>
Search lost images and reconnect with family pictures.

2. Family Web pages

Enter your family surnames into a search engine like <www.google.com> to locate family pages or use the SuperSearch feature of the *Family Tree Magazine* Web site <www.familytree magazine.com>. In addition to using your surname, try searching, for example, "Taylor genealogy" or "Taylor Family History." Use the special image search features on <www.google.com> or <www.altavista.com> specifically for photographs.

3. Auctions

Use online auctions such as <www.eBay.com> to purchase items that relate to your family. Enter your surname or a place name and see what happens.

4. Message boards

Communicating with other people of the same surname via <www.Gen Forum.com> and similar sites can uncover additional genealogical information and photographs. (See Chapter 1 for a list.)

Look in the Library

Picture research can require a visit to a large research facility—in person at a museum, public or university library, or historical society; or virtually via the Internet. Most large museums have libraries, and many offer research hours to the public. Be sure to ask about special bibliographies and indexes, and tap resources such as:

● *Printed material:* Don't overlook printed materials such as magazines and books as sources of pictures. If your ancestors gained recognition in their chosen field, their successes, complete with a picture, might be recorded in a professional journal. If they graduated from high school or college, check yearbooks for images. Students have posed for portraits since Samuel Morse took the first class portrait of the Yale class of 1840.

● *Newspapers:* If your ancestor participated in a local or national event, it may have appeared in print. To hunt for ancestral descriptions in early newspapers, you can tap online newspaper databases such as Accessible Archives <www.accessible.com> or Ancestry's Historical Newspaper Collection <www.ancestry.com/search/rectype/periodicals/news/main.htm?lfl=ttd>. For microfilmed archives of local newspapers, the United States Newspaper Project <www.neh.fed.us/projects/usnp.html> is a good starting place. Newspapers started publishing photographs as engravings in the 1860s, and later in the century had the technology to print actual photographs. Unfortunately, most newspaper collections are unindexed, so it's difficult to find a person unless you already have a date associated with a particular event. Obituary notices weren't accompanied by images until the 1900s.

● *Biographical encyclopedias:* Another good source of photographs is subscription publications, also known as

SPECIAL LIBRARIES AND ARCHIVES FOR FINDING IMAGES ON THE WEB

American Memory Project
←memory.loc.gov→
Search by collection or the entire group of seven million digitized records.

Francis Frith Collection
←www.francisfrith.com→
Search this online collection of images taken by Frith & Co. between 1860 and 1970 of British towns and villages.

Getty Research Institute
←www.getty.edu/research/library→
The institute developed the Art and Architecture Thesaurus and the Union List of Artists' Names. You can search their databases through an online catalog.

Library of Congress Prints and Photographs Division
←www.loc.gov/rr/print→
Approximately 50 percent of the Library's holdings are accessible through the online catalog.

Making of America
←moa.umdl.umich.edu→
Search online digitized books and journals from the Antebellum period through Reconstruction.

National Portrait Gallery
←www.npg.si.edu→
Search by subject of the painting and then look for biographical data. You can specify the artistic medium you're looking for—painting, engraving, caricature, etc.

Otherdays.com
←www.otherdays.com→
Use the online digital library of photographs from the Lawrence Collection (1870-1910) or print and drawing galleries for scenes of Ireland.

Steamship Historical Society of America
←www.ubalt.edu/archives/ship/transe.htm→
University of Baltimore Library, 1420 Maryland Ave., Baltimore, MD 21201
The Society maintains an archive of photographs of ships that brought immigrants to America. Write for information and then order copies of relevant images.

United States Army Military History Institute
←Carlisle-www.army.mil/usamhi/photoDB.html→
Write to Special Collections, 22 Ashburn Dr., Carlisle, PA 17013. Use the Web site and archive to find photographs of military participation.

"mug books." Popular in the nineteenth century, these books provided biographical sketches of prominent citizens of a particular area. A portrait of the person usually accompanied the biography.

• *Family genealogies:* Unfortunately, there is no index to illustrations that appear in published genealogies, but the family histories themselves are easy to find with a list of surnames and accessibility to a major genealogical collection in your area. While genealogies didn't regularly include portraits until the mid- to late-nineteenth century, you might find some earlier prints in more recent publications. Check the frontispiece of each genealogy that relates to your family name to see if illustrations were used. Online catalog listings may also sometimes note whether there are illustrations.

TRY HISTORICAL SOCIETIES

When you start your search, include a list of all the places your ancestors lived, their occupations, and any record of military service. By checking the photograph collection in the small historical societies in places where your ancestors lived, you can uncover images of the town and possibly of your ancestors. Estates often donate identified photograph collections to these institutions.

If you live a long distance from these societies, send a brief letter of inquiry about whether they have a collection of photographs and what their policies are on searching for a few individuals. If your search is successful, there will be a fee to reproduce the image. Longer lists will require you to hire an independent researcher in the area. (See the list of state historical societies in the Appendix.)

Re-examine any family papers you've accumulated. Work passes, badges, identification cards, passports, and naturalization certificates are more likely to contain pictures. You can even find pictures in prison records, court documents, and police files.

PHOTO PERMISSIONS

Whether you are creating a scrapbook or adding to your family photograph collection, there are things you need to know about photo permissions. You're probably thinking, it's just a scrapbook, why do I have to know about photo permissions? As long as the scrapbook is just for personal use, you're fine, but if you decide to publish your scrapbook as a book or even online, make sure you know about photo permissions. The time to check is before you use an image in your scrapbook, rather than later. Photographs with a copyright notice or that appear in a book may need special permission to copy. If in doubt, consult the copyright table on the Library of Congress' Web site <lcweb.loc.gov/copyright/title17>.

Here are a couple of good reasons:
• A relative uses a photograph of you having a bad moment in a scrapbook and gives copies of the album to relatives as presents. You didn't give your permission to include the photograph.

• You decide to publish your heritage scrapbook, in which you've used published illustrations still under copyright. The photographer sues you.

These are not unusual instances. It is best to know the facts before proceeding. In fact, a little pre-planning will save you trouble later on.

Using photographs and other images is a complicated issue. There are public domain images you can use for free, but in some cases they are in private collections, and the owner will charge you a royalty fee for usage. So when is a photograph in the public domain? It depends on several factors, including whether the photograph is unique, if it has been published, and the creation date. Keep in mind that a photograph does not require a copyright symbol to be protected under the law.

According to copyright law, a photographer is considered the "author" or creator of photographic works and as such is the legal copyright holder. If you want to make photographic copies of a photograph, alter it, or publish it, you need the photographer's permission to do so. You need to proceed carefully when using old images and other illustrations rather than assuming they are in the public domain, which means they are free to use.

If you want to use a photograph taken or published after 1978, obtaining permission can be a simple procedure as long as you can contact the current copyright holder. Send the photographer a letter requesting permission and outlining how the image will be used. In most cases, you will have to pay a royalty (usage fee) for the right to publish the image. As long as you are just using an image in a scrapbook and not publishing it in print or online this won't be an issue.

THE PUBLIC DOMAIN

Here's the situation if you decide to publish a historical family photograph. While historical materials published prior to 1923 are in the public domain, the issue of use is still complex. Before you use any historical images, determine if they were ever published, i.e. made available for general distribution to the public, and when the photographer died. Under the 1978 law, unpublished materials created prior to 1923, including photographs, are covered by special rules. If the images were published after

1978, then they are under copyright for an additional 45 years or at least until December 31, 2047. Suppose you purchase an original image at an antique store. It was never published, the photographer is dead, and it is unidentified. Can you use it? If the image or item was created prior to 1923 then it may be in the public domain. If not, evaluate the risk in using unpublished images based on their economic value and the risk of being discovered. In many cases where the copyright status is uncertain, you may be able to safely use the picture in a publication or online. A scrapbook is considered personal use unless you decide to print copies or publish it. When in doubt, contact an attorney for reassurance.

Suppose you find a family photograph in an archive or historical society? There are also ethical concerns with historical images found in museum collections. Since you probably won't want to use just a photocopy of this image, you'll approach the museum or archive about making a photographic copy. You'll have to pay a fee for this service and tell them how it will be used.

If you decide to publish the image in print or online, you may have to pay a usage fee. Even though many of these images are in the public domain, the museum can license you to use them and charge a fee. If it is a unique item, then you should pay the fee (they vary from institution to institution); however, if the photograph was published prior to 1923 and unaltered copies are available in other institutions, then they are in the public domain.

FAMILY PHOTOGRAPHS

If you want to use a family photograph taken by a professional photographer, the copyright issues remain the same. Photographers hold the copyright for images; therefore, you cannot publish

GENERAL RULES TO FOLLOW WHEN USING IMAGES

• Make sure you have permission of the owner to use the image in your scrapbook.
• If you decide to publish your scrapbook online or as a book, follow the copyright rules previously outlined.
• Images published before 1923 are in the public domain and can be used.

RULES OF CARING FOR IMAGES

Golden Rule: Don't do anything to your photographs that can't be undone.

DO'S AND DON'TS FOR PHOTOGRAPHS
(See Chapters 8 and 9 for more handling and storage suggestions.)

Do's
1. Use acid- and lignin-free paper and polypropylene or Mylar sleeves.
2. Display copy photos, placing originals in storage.
3. Identify the pictures.
4. Consult a professional conservator for damaged images
5. Store them in an area with stable temperature and humidity, such as a windowless closet.

Don'ts
1. Don't use magnetic albums with adhesive pages.
2. Never crop original photographs.
3. Never write on the front of images
4. Don't place adhesive directly on an image or attach cutouts
5. Don't store photographs in attics, basements, or unstable environments.

any professional studio photographs of relatives without permission. In order for professional photographers to use your image in advertising or publications they also need a release from you beforehand. Reprints of releases and an explanation of rights appear in the *ASMP Guide to Professional Practices in Photography* (Allworth Press, 2001). Several professional organizations including the Professional Photographers of America have agreed to adhere to a set of copyright guidelines outlined by the Photo Marketing Association International. A complete set of the responsibilities of the consumer and professional photographers is on the Kodak Web site <www.kodak.com/global/en/consumer/doingMore/copyright.shtml> or in the *ASMP Guide to Professional Practices in Photography*.

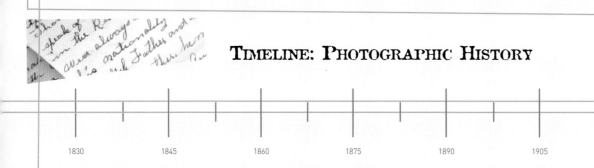

TIMELINE: PHOTOGRAPHIC HISTORY

1830	1845	1860	1875	1890	1905

1839
A patent is issued to Louis Daguerre for a method of capturing images on metal.

1840
Francois Gouraud visits America to demonstrate the daguerreotype process. The first daguerreotype studio opens in New York City that same year.

1850
Mathew Brady publishes his Gallery of Illustrious Americans. It contains portraits and biographies of eminent American citizens.

1853
Tintype introduced by Hamilton L. Smith of Ohio.

1854
James Ambrose Cutting is issued a patent for the ambrotype.

1856
Alexander Gardner introduces a process for making photographic enlargements.

1857
The Duke of Parma introduces the carte de visite.

1859
Carte de visites are brought to America.

1861
First patent issued for a photograph album.

1864-66
Revenue stamps are required for photographs.

1868
H.M. Crider introduces photographic marriage certificates.

1884
Flashlight photography using magnesium light is introduced.

1888
Kodak roll film camera introduced.

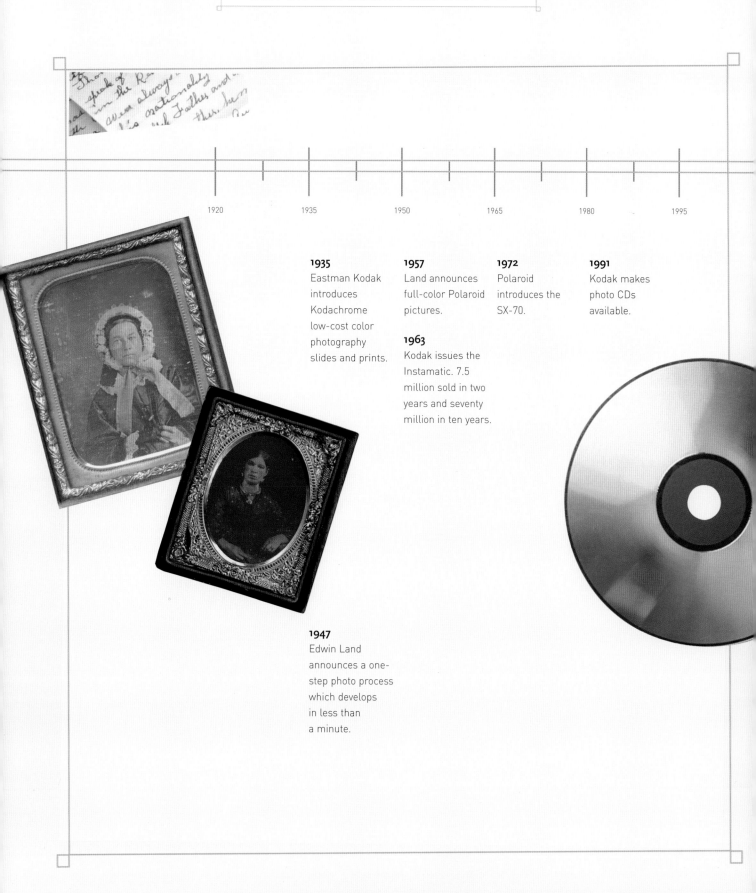

1920 · 1935 · 1950 · 1965 · 1980 · 1995

1935
Eastman Kodak
introduces
Kodachrome
low-cost color
photography
slides and prints.

1957
Land announces
full-color Polaroid
pictures.

1972
Polaroid
introduces the
SX-70.

1991
Kodak makes
photo CDs
available.

1963
Kodak issues the
Instamatic. 7.5
million sold in two
years and seventy
million in ten years.

1947
Edwin Land
announces a one-
step photo process
which develops
in less than
a minute.

CHAPTER THREE

WORKING WITH DOCUMENTS

My husband works with computers, not old documents. One night as I sat transcribing a census page, he glanced over and cried, "How can you read that?" He had no idea how to decipher old handwriting. In fact, he was totally unable to read it. I reassured him that the more you read older documents, the more familiar you become with the handwriting style. It does, however, require patience to learn to read and transcribe unfamiliar script and to understand the clues in a manuscript such as those listed in the sidebar on page 54.

While we all learned handwriting in school, our signature often departs from that practiced lettering. That's why graphologists claim that handwriting analysis provides insight into the personality of the writer. But there are also family history hints in a person's handwriting. For instance, penmanship can establish a time period for a document, the educational level of the person who wrote it, and the identity of the writer. You can discover new things about your family through their handwriting and enhance your scrapbook with information about writing styles. Including handwriting samples in your heritage album is another visual way of connecting to your ancestors. Imagine finding a diary written by an ancestor and then including copies of those entries next to photographs of them. Suddenly, you're telling a story with both words and pictures.

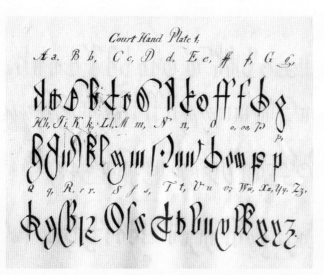

Alphabet in the Court Hand from a copy book, "Exposition of Latin Words." New England Historic Genealogical Society.

LEARN THE HISTORY

Today we equate literacy with being able to read and write, but in earlier centuries writing was taught separately from reading. Being able to sign your name did not mean that you had attended formal school. Reading was important to study the Bible, but writing wasn't essential. Officials wrote documents and men who couldn't write signed their mark, a design that distinguished them from others. A signature of full name was not required. In Colonial America, individuals could enroll in private writing classes as early as 1684, or use self-teaching manuals. In the eighteenth and nineteenth centuries, penmanship masters traveled around the country teaching the fine art of handwriting to persons wanting to sign their name or to young women using penmanship as artistic expression. Writing reflected economic affluence and for businessmen, clergy, and public officials, it was necessary to be able to write. Reading and writing as indicators of literacy is a twentieth-century concept. Questions regarding an individual's skill in reading and writing continued as separate columns on the United States census until 1930.

Handwriting is not only different for each generation of your family tree, but it is also a reflection of the writing technology available at the time. The shape and style of the pen nib influenced the development of new handwriting methods. For example, it is difficult to create certain scripts with a flat pen nib. You can do an informal study of twentieth century handwriting methods by asking relatives to write the alphabet on separate sheets of paper and comparing them. While individuals tend to develop their own style regardless of the method taught in school, certain letter formations will let you identify when they were taught to write and in what script.

RECOGNIZE THE STYLE

As you become familiar with different types of handwriting, you can set an undated document into a time frame and learn more about the person who wrote the words. In Colonial America the majority of the population learned one style of handwriting, but well-educated individuals often learned several different methods of script or hands. Men and women often learned different hands, so that someone familiar with a variety of scripts would be able to identify the sex of the writer from the handwriting. The same was true for social status. Private secretaries wrote in a particular style while their employers would sign in another, thus establishing that they did not write the document. Different calligraphic styles of script—Gothic, Italian, Secretary and Roundhand—co-existed in Colonial America. Not until the late nineteenth century did one particular handwriting method become dominant in the United States.

Italian
The script we call Italics is also the Italian hand. Instead of the block letters of the Gothic script, Italian has rounded letter formations. Queen Elizabeth of England used cursive Italian script in her writings.

Secretary or Court Hand: Seventeenth century
Known by multiple names including Secretary, Court Hand, and Gothic, this is the most common script that researchers encounter in materials from the seventeenth century. Some early American handwriting also called Mayflower Century script is a combination of Secretary, Italic and, by the turn of the seventeenth century, Roundhand. In part, American script reflects the handwriting style of early English immigrants.

Roundhand: 1700-1840
As copy books or self-teaching handwriting manuals began to be printed by copper plate engraving, a style known as Roundhand became popular and helped introduce new writing implements so that the fine script could be duplicated. It is recognizable by its thin upstrokes and thicker downstrokes.

Spencerian: 1865-1890

In the nineteenth century a new style appeared— Spencerian. It was a uniquely American handwriting system derived from three competing penmanship masters. Characterized by flourishes, it reflected the feminine pursuits of the Victorian period. Writing was a slow process because of the number of loops and times the pen lifted from the page to form letters. Spencerian handwriting became the dominant method of script in the late nineteenth century, taught in schools and in copybooks.

Palmer: 1880-1960s

The developer of the Palmer method thought his script plain, legible, and suited to the fast pace of business rather than the slow pen strokes of the Spencerian method. Ask your parents or grandparents about the movement drills practiced in the classroom.

D'Nealian: 1965-present

If you have children or grandchildren currently learning to write, this is probably what they are being taught. The letters in the printed version of D'Nealian help children learn manuscript writing without learning different letter formations.

Stylistic Variations

If you've ever tried to read a seventeenth-century document or earlier, you know the frustrations of handwriting. It can be like learning another language. In fact, there are several things you can encounter.

Handwriting Difficulties

Illegible handwriting can be the result of many factors including improper instruction, illness, or even evidence of learning disabilities. In earlier centuries, pupils learned writing through the use of copybooks, requiring students to exactly duplicate the letters and style shown. If schooling wasn't completed, penmanship lacked the discipline of the

"A Treatise of Fortification" written in copperplate by David Mason, c. 1755. New England Historic Genealogical Society.

Class at St. Edwards School, Providence, RI, c. 1900. Rhode Island Historical Society.

Membership application for Charles E. Tucker in Spencerian script. New England Historic Genealogical Society.

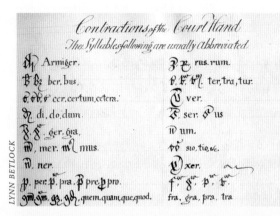

"Contractions of the Court Hand" is a table to help researchers understand that shorthand used in documents. New England Historic Genealogical Society.

repetitious practicing. Evidence of certain types of medical conditions and old age appear as tremulous writing with shaky letter formation. Dysgraphia, a type of learning disability, also appears as illegible handwriting. It can indicate dyslexia. A famous example of a writing disability is Leonardo DaVinci's mirror writing.

Shorthand and Abbreviations
A type of shorthand frustrates researchers trying to use the letters of Roger Williams, one of the original founders of Rhode Island. To this day, many of his notes remain indecipherable. If you find self-created shorthand in family papers, the writer probably utilized it to expedite the writing process and possibly confuse anyone trying to sneak a peak at a diary or letter. Abbreviations are a type of shorthand. Some standard ones appear in official documents while others are individual adaptations. When trying to decipher shorthand or abbreviations it helps to create a reference chart of these idiosyncrasies for each manuscript.

Spelling
Having only one way to spell a word is a twentieth-century concept related to widely available free public schooling and mandatory education laws. If you can't figure out a word once you've transcribed it, try saying it aloud. It might be a phonetic spelling of a word.

Archaic Words or Phrases
Older documents often contain words and phrases that are unfamiliar. In these cases, a word may have a different definition or have fallen out of general usage. Consulting the Oxford English Dictionary or a dictionary from the time period of the document will usually explain the meaning. There are also genealogical dictionaries such as *A to Zax* by Barbara Jean Evans (Hearthside Press, 1995) that are compilations of unusual words and phrases commonly found in materials used by family historians.

Signum or Mark
Before individuals learned to sign their name, they left their "mark." Also known as a signum, these unique symbols identified specific individuals. Each sign is usually accompanied by the words "his mark." The use of signs declined as the population learned to write.

STYLES

Left-handedness
While not all left-handed individuals write with a backward slant, penmanship with that feature can indicate a person's dominant hand. There is one caution: At least one writing master in the mid-nineteenth century purposefully taught his pupils to write with a backward slant.

Flourishes
Some writing instructors taught pupils to create artistic works with penmanship. Using the same pen strokes used for letter formation, students could draw birds and borders with pen flourishes for graphic interest.

Writing instructors often taught pupils to use handwriting to decorate documents. Order Book for the Massachusetts Militia, 1st division, 3rd brigade, 1822-1844. New England Historic Genealogical Society.

The signature of John Accars (no dates). New England Historic Genealogical Society.

Fraktur

Decorated writings of the Pennsylvania German Folk art tradition, called Fraktur, began appearing in Germany, Alsace, and Switzerland in the early seventeenth century. It most commonly appears on certificates for births and baptisms and in family records for immigrants from those areas.

DECIPHERING HANDWRITING

Now that you are aware of the challenges and pitfalls you can start working on that puzzling document. You may never become totally fluent in transcribing a particular style of handwriting, but you can learn enough to discover data and reveal names. Researchers completely unfamiliar with deciphering handwriting should spend time reading manuals created by expert genealogists and by following their methods.

Immigration Clues

The handwriting styles discussed here are American versions. Penmanship styles differ in other countries and cultures. If you are trying to read script from someone who did not learn the technique in this country, there will be variations in letter formation and usually in the way certain numbers appear. Handwriting can help verify that the person immigrated to the United States after learning to write in his country of origin.

Compare

Different styles of handwriting have certain idiosyncrasies that can lead to transcription errors. For instance seventeenth-century documents written in secretary hand are full of abbreviations and letter formations that look strange to us today. In roundhand *s* is formed by a long flourish that is often confused with a *p* or an *f*. Spend time

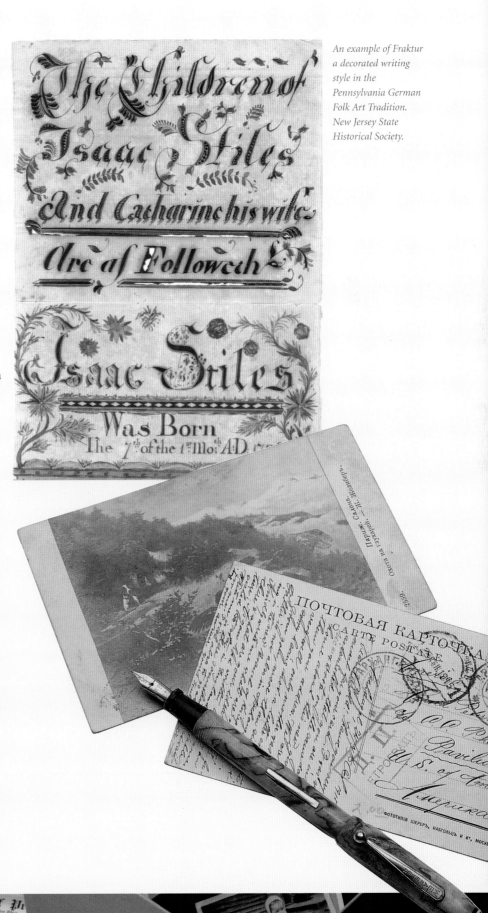

An example of Fraktur a decorated writing style in the Pennsylvania German Folk Art Tradition. New Jersey State Historical Society.

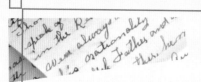

DATING AN UNDATED MANUSCRIPT

So, can you establish a time frame for an undated document? The answer is yes, but it can be difficult. Try answering these questions.

1. What is the style of handwriting?

First try to identify the handwriting style to provide a general sense of when the document was written. Don't forget to compare the penmanship to other records possibly written by the same person.

2. Is there a watermark?

Hold the sheet of paper up to the light. Watermarks are set into the paper and identify the paper manufacturer. If there is one you can then research that company at a large public library to see when that particular watermark was used.

3. What type of paper is it?

Various styles of paper became fashionable at different dates, so examine the sheet of paper for color, edging, and size. For example, parchment paper was not manufactured in the United States until 1885.

4. What was used to create the document?

Other factors such as type of pen or pencil, ink erasure marks, and even drying sand and blotters help you learn more about the document in your hands. Certain styles of pen nibs became popular at various times, so by comparing the undated document to another dated one from the same person may help you judge when it was created. See Joe Nickell's book Pen, Ink, & Evidence: *A Study of Writing and Writing Materials for the Penman, Collector, and Document Detective* for a history of writing implements.

5. Does a stamp appear on the document?

Postage stamps and wax seals can reveal a date for a document.

6. Still having trouble?

Consult a professional. If establishing a date becomes important, contact the American Society of Questioned Document Examiners. The society maintains a referral list of members on its Web site ← www.asqde.org/abrefpg.htm→.

poring over a document, looking at each word, and identifying all the capital and lower case letters that you are sure of. When you find a letter that is indecipherable, try comparing it to other words in the manuscript until you find similarities. There will be times when this doesn't work, but in many cases you can locate an approximate match. Deciphering each document letter by letter creates a stylistic alphabet chart and builds your self-confidence.

Context

There are almost always words that will scare you with their illegibility. When this happens, step back from the word and read the rest of the document to see if you can pick up any contextual clues.

Have Patience

Sometimes trying to read an old document takes hours or even days. While you want to be able to read it as easily as the words in this book, it may not be possible. You wouldn't expect to learn Greek in an afternoon, so why set yourself up for failure by rushing the process. When you become frustrated, set the document aside for a day or two, until you are ready to try again.

Overcoming Obstacles

It may not be a problem with the handwriting that stops you from completely understanding a document. Physical deterioration in the form of faded ink, water damage, or worn documents can obscure single letters or even whole paragraphs. My ancestors almost always end up on a census page smeared from exposure to water. Older inks have a tendency to fade. Ultraviolet light can help you read faded ink. Ask other researchers how they overcome these difficult roadblocks.

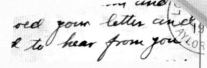

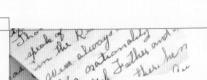

TIPS FROM EMILY ANNE CROOM IN UNPUZZLING YOUR PAST (Betterway Books, 2001)

- Lower case letters *u*, *n*, *w* and *m* often look alike
- Watch out for undotted *i*'s and uncrossed *t*'s.
- Words with double *s*'s can appear to be *ʃs* or *ps*.
- Capital letters *S*, *L*, and *T* can have a similar appearance.
- *I* and *J* look the same.

Heritage Album Tip:

Ask family members to sign their name under their photographs so that you have a record of their handwriting. Don't forget to add a sample of your own penmanship by including some handwritten journaling.

FOUR STEPS TO SUCCESSFUL TRANSCRIPTION

- Do create a reference chart of letters for each document.
- Do compare script and study the context of difficult words.
- Don't try to rush, take your time.
- Do consult with others.

TYPES OF HANDWRITTEN DOCUMENTS

- Bible records
- Diaries
- Letters
- Genealogical notes
- Census
- Immigration and passenger documents
- Business records
- Recipes
- Any paper work prepared by hand

NEW ENGLAND HISTORIC GENEALOGICAL SOCIETY

RESOURCES

Books

- *Handwriting of American Records for 300 Years* by E. Kay Kirkham (Everton Publishers, 1973)

- *Handwriting in America: A Cultural History* by Tamara Plakins Thornton (Yale University Press, 1996)

- *Pen, Ink, & Evidence: A Study of Writing and Writing Materials for the Penman, Collector, and Document Detective* by Joe Nickell (Oak Knoll Books, 2002)

- *Reading Early American Handwriting* by Kip Sperry (Genealogical Publishing Co., 1998)

- *Organizing and Preserving Your Heirloom Documents* by Katherine Scott Sturdevant (Betterway Books, 2002).

Web sites

- *The Fraktur Tradition* <www.region.waterloo.on.ca/Jsh2> Learn more about Fraktur and look at a few examples. Click on "Collections," then "Fraktur."

FIND ANOTHER OPINION

If you've tried without success to read a document, enlist the help of another researcher or other professional with manuscript experience. What you found difficult they may be able to read effortlessly, but there are times when even the experts have trouble.

Reading an old family letter or diary is a bit like time travel. You have a sense of what your ancestors experienced in their words. Deciphering old penmanship can seem too frustrating to be worth it, but it only takes one discovery to prove how valuable that skill can become. As any researcher knows,

finding a first name or middle initial can change the course of genealogical research and lead to new discoveries.

FINDING FAMILY MANUSCRIPTS

When Ken Burns used one of Sullivan Ballou's letters in the PBS production *The Civil War* there were probably gasps in living rooms across America. Why? Because some Ballou family members probably didn't realize that one of their ancestors left such poignant letters. As the media buzz started over his romantic words, librarians at the Rhode Island Historical Society decided to look at the Ballou material in their collection. As it turns out, there were a few more letters from him to his wife Sarah.

While your ancestor may not have left such a powerful group of manuscripts— letters, diaries and other papers—it may help you learn about the daily lives of your relatives. Have you ever wondered if your ancestors left any written record? You may own small groups of letters or even a diary, but there may be more material sitting in archives and libraries that you are unaware of. At one point, looking for manuscripts involved hours of checking indexes, but online offerings have streamlined the process. Before you start looking, it helps to understand the basic vocabulary used by archivists and librarians.

- *Inventory:* Historical background on the subject of the papers; what material is in the collection; list of file folders and sometimes if there are other family-related collections in the same archive. Inventories can be several pages long or a short paragraph.

- *Provenance:* Information on the past owners of the material in the collection.

- *Record Group:* A group of related records based on provenance. Some

archives keep manuscripts and photographs in a record group, but that is not the case in all repositories.

Basically, your goal is to attempt to find everything associated with your ancestor such as diaries, letters, and family papers, because every piece of paper provides additional details of their life. It's helpful to remember that whether or not you find material depends, in part, on your ancestor's gender and level of literacy. Men generally left more written evidence behind. You might not find letters written by your great-great-grandmother but you might be surprised by what can be discovered about her in the manuscripts written by other relatives. Even if you don't succeed in the beginning, keep looking.

Ask Relatives

What's the number one way people locate family papers? Through family members—those you know and distant relatives. Track down all your relatives and ask if they own anything that belonged to ancestor X or Y or if they have anything with your ancestor's handwriting? So that they don't hang up immediately or slam the door in your face, make sure you preface your question with some background on your search for family history. Offering to make copies of the information you have gathered can lead to reciprocal sharing.

Message Boards

Not all manuscripts get donated; many remain in private collections, so using message boards is still one of the best ways to broadcast a family search. Post a message on a surname or geographic board and see if anyone in the network has manuscripts for your ancestor. If you own papers, then you might want to add that to your posting and offer to share material. Never mail original documents; make copies and send those.

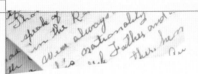

SKILL-BUILDING: WRITING A QUERY TO A HISTORICAL SOCIETY OR PRIVATE ARCHIVE

Be Understanding:

Rather than expecting an answer in a record amount of time (because the Internet is faster), understand that historical societies are struggling with the increase in requests. Since the majority of these societies are understaffed, the burden on existing staff has driven several societies not to accept e-mail research queries.

Remember Your Letter-Writing Skills:

Just because e-mail communication is more informal than regular letter writing doesn't mean you don't have to pay attention to the details. A person who expects (and often receives) an answer to an e-mail sends a well-constructed and thoughtful message. Make sure your inquiry includes the following:

• Your name—include your full first and last names (many e-mail requests only contain a first name or nickname).
• The name of the person you are researching—in order for researchers to assess your request, they need to know the name of the person you are researching.

• When he or she lived and died—if you don't know an exact date of birth, death, or marriage, an approximate date can be helpful.
• Where he or she lived—since very few names are unique, it is important to know not only when a person lived, but where.
• The exact information you are looking for and why—a brief explanation can save time and money.
• A list of sources already consulted—researchers want to know what types of research you have tried already and whether it was successful. A short list of that material with author and title is appreciated.
• A regular mailing address and telephone number—sounds simple, yet many e-mails lack even the bare essentials of full name and address. In the time it takes an organization to respond, you may have changed your e-mail address. Some material is not available over the Internet and will have to be mailed to you.
• A thank you—always express your gratitude for the time it took to answer your letter. Everyone likes to be appreciated for the work they do.

Make Appropriate Inquiries:

In order to increase the odds of receiving a reply to your e-mail, make sure that your inquiry is appropriate. In other words, use the Internet or books to find out what materials are available at various institutions before you write. Several Web sites including Cyndi's List ←www.cyndis-list.com→ and the US GenWeb ←www.USGenWeb.org→ are good ways to investigate the holdings of research facilities. You can also do that by checking the Web site of the historical society you want to contact. Only a few state historical societies don't have a Web site at this writing. See the list of State Historical Societies and their e-mail policies in the Appendix.

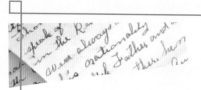

CARING FOR YOUR DOCUMENTS

- Remove staples, paper clips, rubber bands, and metal fasteners from documents. They deteriorate and cause damage.
- Handle documents as little as possible and wear cotton gloves.
- Store flat in acid- and lignin-free enclosures, such as folders, and certain types of plastics, such as Mylar.
- Never laminate documents.
- Keep them in a dark place with a stable temperature and humidity.
- Let professionals repair and de-acidify documents.
- Include original documents in your heritage album only if they are encapsulated (see page 62) and you follow the safe scrapbooking guidelines in Chapter 8.

Online Search Engines

Try entering your ancestor's name into a search engine such as Google <www.google.com> and see what turns up. You might discover an online transcription or a collection in a private library. Unfortunately, if your ancestor had a common name like John Brown, you'll encounter more sites than you want to look at. Try narrowing down the possibilities by adding a geographic place after the name.

Archival Collections

Even if you own some of your ancestor's personal documents, try using the Library of Congress's National Union Catalog of Manuscript Collections NUCMC) (either online <www.loc.gov/coll/nucmc/nucmc.html> or in printed volumes). On this site you'll find a directory of manuscripts and archives in the United States. This is a list of organizations that submit information to NUCMC. According to the Web site, printed volumes 1-29 (1959-1993) contain descriptions of more than 72,000 collections in close to 1,500 repositories indexed by subject and family, corporate, and geographic names. If you can't locate the volumes at a library near you, it is possible to order microfilm copies (thirty-five dollars per reel) from the Library of Congress, Photoduplication Service, 101 Independence Ave. SE, Washington, DC 20540-5230.

If your public library system participates in publisher Chadwyck-Healey's online publication, ArchivesUSA, then you have easy access to NUCMC cataloging from 1959 to the present. Chadwyck-Healey has also published the *Index to Personal Names in the National Union Catalog of Manuscript Collections, 1959-1984* (2 vols., 1988), and the *Index to Subjects and Corporate Names in the National Union Catalog of Manuscript Collections, 1959-1984* (3 vols., 1994). ArchivesUSA is a directory of more than five thousand archives in the United States. Each repository listing provides complete contact information, collecting policies, and URLs (Web addresses).

Write a letter or e-mail the local historical society in the area in which your ancestor lived about searching the collections for appropriate material. They might charge a search fee, but if they find something it will be worth the investment. You can try calling first or check the home page to find out about research policies. Even some small public libraries maintain collections of material. An excellent guide to libraries is the *American Library Association American Library Directory* (R.R. Bowker, 2001-2002).

Auctions

If you haven't tried participating in an online or even local auction, don't hesitate. There is a tremendous amount of material for sale including personal letters, diaries, and even city and town records. If you decide to use <www.eBay.com>, there are plenty of user-friendly features such as automatic bidding (you set the limit). You can even take online tutorials on buying, selling, and how eBay works. There are plenty of search options: select a specific category such as "Antiques" or try all listings at one time. For instance, type your surname into the search engine in a particular category and see what might turn up for sale. Believe it or not, it is possible to purchase "lost" family documents over the Internet.

Reunion Sites

Just as there are sites to reunite people with missing photographs, there are a couple that include manuscripts. To keep up to date, look at <www.cyndis list.com> under the categories "Diaries and Letters" and "Family Bibles."

• *Past Connect*
<www.pastconnect.com>
A database of items—letters, diplomas, marriage certificates, etc.—found at auctions, estate sales, flea markets, yard sales, and from other sources.

• *Ford & Nagle*
<my.erinet.com/~fordnag/Ford Nagle.htm>
They've posted family Bibles, documents, and photographs they have found and want to reunite with family members.

PRESERVATION SOLUTIONS

A majority of people clip obituaries, news items, vital record announcements, and even advertisements from newspapers for their informational content. The problem is storing those clippings for the future. Newspapers are a great resource, but the durability of those clippings depends on both the type of paper and how they are stored.

Paper made before circa 1865 consists of a variety of fibers—cotton, flax, linen, and even some wood pulp. Clippings from newspapers printed on this "rag" paper will last forever with the right storage conditions. Unfortunately, the need to mass produce the news in the nineteenth century meant publishers began using wood pulp alone for newspapers because it was inexpensive. This cheap paper tends to become yellow and brittle over time. Leave a newspaper in the sun as an accelerated aging experiment and by the end of the day it will be yellow. Lignin, a substance found in wood that acts as a natural strengthening agent, combined with the acid found in wood pulp causes deterioration. Acid migration from these wood pulp-based papers will stain photographs, other clippings, and anything else stored with them. Older newspaper clippings that are brown and brittle are showing the tell-tale signs of a wood-based paper. There are several ways you can extend the life span of the clippings in your collection whether they are made from plant fibers or from wood ranging from photocopying to special chemical treatments. Options range from affordable to expensive.

One of the first things you should do to preserve your clippings is identify them, including the name of the newspaper in which they appeared, the date, and the page. That way if the clipping becomes too brittle you can still track down microfilmed copies of the original paper and make new copies. Don't forget to make an extra copy, just in case something happens to the original.

A simple solution is to place your news clippings in acid- and lignin-free folders. This type of storage material is available from a variety of library suppliers such as Hollinger Corp. <www. hollingercorp.com> and Light Impressions <www.lightimpressions direct.com/servlet/OnlineShopping>. Before placing them in folders, be sure to remove all paper clips (which rust) and rubber bands (which deteriorate). See Chapter 8 for information on including these items in a scrapbook.

Place those folders in an environment with a stable temperature and humidity (77 degrees Fahrenheit and 50 percent humidity). Fluctuations of those two factors can accelerate deterioration. Damp conditions like those

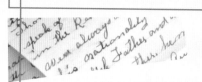

REPAIRING A TORN MANUSCRIPT OR BOOK

- Encapsulate a document to protect it from future damage.
- Do not use standard tape; instead purchase the pressure-sensitive mending tape used in archives and sold by vendors such as University Products (see Appendix).

DE-ACIDIFYING DOCUMENTS

The acid content in most papers and documents will hasten the deterioration and also turn the paper yellow. This can be eliminated by a de-acidification process, which neutralizes the acids in the papers. (It's not necessary for photographs.) If you're encapsulating documents and want to de-acidify them, you can place a piece of buffered paper (available through most archival supply catalogs) under the document first. The only problem with the addition of the buffered paper is that it will keep you from being able to view both sides of a double-sided document.

found in basements and attics encourage mold and mildew. Insects and rodents like to use paper for nests or food, so carefully select a storage area in your house. One man stored all of his genealogical material in a barn. As you can imagine, sorting through those papers required a mask and a good pair of gloves as shields from droppings and mold. There was even a little hay mixed in with the papers. The newspaper clippings were in the worst shape due to spending years in an unstable environment. A good storage location in your house is an interior windowless closet away from heat, light and water.

You can stop the acid deterioration of clippings by using a de-acidification solution used by professional conservators. It can be purchased through "archival" suppliers and in some scrapbook stores. "Archival" is a general term that actually has no industry standards. For this reason, be cautious when using any item labeled "archival" without first finding out if in fact it will cause any damage to your clippings or other materials. Conservators advise trying the process on a small section of a newspaper to test the solubility of inks. Several brands of de-acidification chemicals are on the market as sprays or solutions including Archival Mist, Bookkeeper and Wei T'O. University Products <www. archivalsuppliers.com> sells a variety of these products as well as a brochure and an instructional video on how to use them. Magnesium oxide is the key ingredient in both Archival Mist and Bookkeeper, both of which are odorless. Users need to spray both sides of a clipping to de-acidify it. Wei T'O comes in a variety of solutions for sensitive or soluble inks or thicker papers. Some of these solutions emit fumes. It is advisable to order the free brochure on using this product before trying it. Solutions require immersion of a clip-

ping rather than a quick spray.

A commonly held belief is that laminating documents preserves them. Actually the opposite it true. Placing a news clipping or anything else between two pieces of plastic will speed up the deterioration and the laminating materials cause additional damage. For the sake of your originals, never laminate them. If you want to protect them from damage due to handling, de-acidify them and encapsulate them by placing them between two sheets of polypropylene plastic or Mylar sleeves with a strip of acid-free adhesive. You can seal all sides or leave one open.

Of course another option is scanning the clippings and printing them on acid- and lignin-free paper. You can purchase long-lasting inks that will work with inkjet printers from Lyson <lyson.com> or from some photo stores.

The least expensive solution of all is to photocopy clippings using acid- and lignin-free paper. It can be difficult to find appropriate paper at office supply stores so you might have to purchase the paper from one of specialty suppliers mentioned in the Appendix. Free catalogs of all their products are available online or through the mail.

TIMELINE OF HANDWRITING

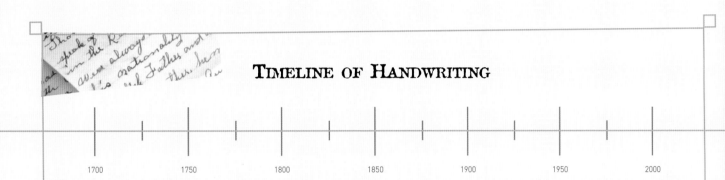

1700   1750   1800   1850   1900   1950   2000

12th century
Paper appears in Europe.

1761
Faber pencil dynasty started by Kaspar Faber.

Late 18th century
Autograph collecting starts as a hobby.

1812
The Art of Judging the Mind and Character of Men and Women from Their Handwriting by Edouard Auguste Patrice Hocquart discusses handwriting analysis.

1867
Typewriter is invented.

1888
Palmer method introduced.

1890-1945
Schools teach several different methods from Palmer, the American Book Company, and Zaner-Bloser. All are characterized by free arm movements.

1894
A.N. Palmer publishes *Palmer's Guide to Business Writing.*

1914
Frank Freeman's *Teaching of Handwriting* introduces scientific penmanship.

1942
American Society of Questioned Document Examiners begins.

1944
United States Army uses ballpoint pens.

1945-present
The ballpoint pen transforms writing by eliminating the need for desks.

1964
D'Nealian script taught in schools.

1979
Paper Mate markets the Eraser Mate Pen.

ENCAPSULATING A DOCUMENT (BY DAVE MISHKIN FROM JUST BLACK & WHITE)

You have several choices for encapsulation. For example, you can purchase plastic sleeves with pockets and slide your photographs into the pockets. There are also other forms of protection you can make or purchase from any archival supply catalog, such as clear, self-sealing envelopes. These forms of encapsulation do offer some protection, but they're not ideal. The best encapsulation method is also one of the easiest: binding two pieces of Mylar together with double-sided archival tape, leaving a tiny "breathing" space. Another advantage to this approach is that it allows you to view both sides.

Although encapsulation looks like lamination, it's a completely different process. You should never laminate a photograph or document under any circumstances. Lamination actually binds the document to the plastic—so it's a destructive process, while encapsulation is a preservation process. When you're ready to start encapsulating, the easiest way to organize your work area is to use a table that you can access from all four sides. If you have to keep turning your work, you may end up having to realign the Mylar pieces several times.

Here's the process, step by step:

1) Cut two polyester (Mylar) sheets of film at least two inches larger than the document or photograph in each direction: top, bottom, left, and right. Do this on grid paper to help you center the object and keep the borders even. (A)

2) Place the first sheet of Mylar on a clean, flat work surface and wipe with a lint-free cloth to remove any dust and to add a static charge. (B)

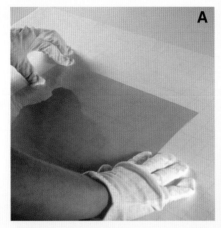

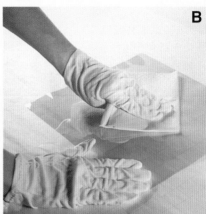

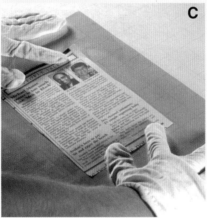

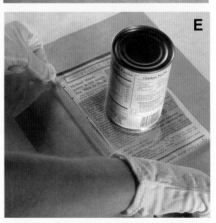

3) Center the document or photograph and place a weight on it to prevent the Mylar from shifting during the encapsulation process. (C and D)

4) Apply the double-sided tape on the Mylar film just below the document. Leave a one-eighth to one-quarter-inch space between the edge of the document and the edge of the tape. Do not remove the brown protective paper on the tape yet. (E)

5) Wipe the second sheet of film with the lint-free cloth to remove any dust and to create a static charge again.

6) Remove the weight from the document and center the new sheet over the document, cleaned side down.

7) Place the weight back on the center of the top Mylar sheet.

8) Lift one corner of the top sheet and carefully remove the brown protective paper along one edge of the document. Lower the corner and rub the film over the tape to adhere it. Then rub the two pieces of Mylar with the brayer where you just taped, to ensure a good seal. (F)

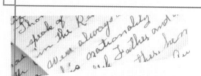

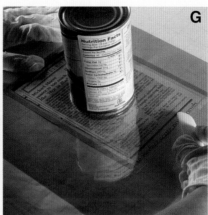

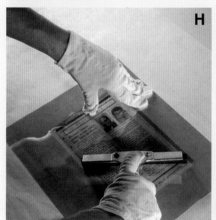

9) Repeat for the other three edges.

10) Don't overlap the tape from one side to the next. Place the tape from one side to the next. Place the tape to almost touch the adjoining side, but be sure not to overlap the tape. When you get to the final corner, leave one-eighth to one-quarter inch of space between the corners to provide a slight "breathing" space.

11) To remove trapped air from between the sheets of Mylar, slide the squeegee from the center of the film out to the edges. (H)

12) Roll the brayer over the tape to bond it firmly to the Mylar.

13) Carefully trim the package, leaving a one-eighth- to one-quarter-inch margin of Mylar outside the tape and

all around the document. Rounding the corners will help prevent scratching or cutting other materials during handling. (I and J)

You'll need to practice this procedure a few times, of course. But once you've mastered this technique, you'll have no problem encapsulating any document or photograph—and protecting your precious keepsakes.

ENCAPSULATION SUPPLY LIST

You'll need the following materials to encapsulate properly and with minimal trouble. Most can be purchased through archival supply catalogs (see Appendix).

- Polyester film Mylar.
- X-acto knife. Olfa is another brand name that has snap-off blades.
- Lint-free cloth, to clean the Mylar and create static electricity.
- Quarter-inch double-stick tape—such as 3M Scotch-brand tape No. 415.
- Ruler.
- Grid paper to help with measurements and to help cut straight lines.
- A weight to hold down the work while you're cutting, sizing and measuring.
- Squeegee to remove the air between the sheets of plastic.
- Brayer to ensure good adhesion and remove excess air.
- Corner cutter (or you can use a sharp, new nail clipper).
- Cotton gloves.

MEMORABILIA, ARTIFACTS, AND HEIRLOOMS

I f you listen closely, you might hear voices emanating from family memorabilia. No, I'm not crazy. Each and every piece of memorabilia, from those baby teeth you've squirreled away to the ticket stubs from the play your grandparents saw on their honeymoon, can come to life in your heritage album with the story it has to tell. Include the stories of any hand-crafted items left in the family such as quilts, holiday ornaments, tablecloths, or toys, by photographing them and using journaling techniques to tell their tale. Sometimes it's the little things our ancestors left behind that tell us something personal about them.

Five Roses
Cook Book

Being a Manual of Good Recipes
carefully chosen from the contributions of over two
thousand successful users of *Five Roses*
Flour throughout Canada

Also

Useful Notes on the various classes of good things
to eat, all of which have been carefully
checked and re-checked by
competent authority

Issued by
Lake of the Woods Milling
Company Limited
Montreal

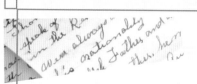

EPHEMERA RESOURCES

**The Ephemera
Society of America, Inc.
Membership Secretary**
P.O. Box 95
Cazenovia, NY 13035-0095
Phone/Fax: (315) 655-9139.
←www.ephemerasociety.org→

*The Encyclopedia of Ephemera: A
Guide to the Fragmentary Documents of
Everyday Life for the Collector, Curator,
and Historian* by Maurice Rickards,
edited and completed by Michael
Twyman with the assistance of Sally
de Beaumont and Amoret Tanenr
(Routledge, 2000)

> **Heritage Album Tip:**
>
> *Make your own scrapbook using cloth covers and special papers—such as vellum or parchment—or use a journal with acid- and lignin-free paper.*

My maternal grandmother raised five children and all that's left are a few things that were important to her—a cookbook with her handwritten notations, a set of ceramic bowls, and her watch. Because she died when I was a baby, the artifacts and family stories have provided me with a sense of knowing her. I can imagine her using the bowls and her cookbook to create some of the recipes my family still makes today, but it's her watch that tells me a story of her life before marriage and children. She bought it with her earnings as a factory worker before she was married and had it engraved with her initials.

What can you learn about an ancestor from one piece of her life? More than you think. Family heirlooms can help fill in the details of your ancestors' lives. Every family has something they collect or a few heirlooms. Watch *Antiques Roadshow* on PBS to see what expert appraisers and antique dealers tell people about their family material that includes both monetary and sentimental value. It's an entertaining way to spend some time before you start rummaging in the attic to see what your ancestors left behind.

Museum curators and archivists catalog all sorts of material identifying these items according to owner, when they were made, and even who they belonged to before the present owner. Let's look at the types of material you can place in a heritage album, what they tell you about your family, and where to locate them. Memorabilia and artifacts are just another piece of the family story—one that is waiting to be discovered and told. So what do you own? Are there stories about certain family artifacts? Where can you discover more?

The types of memorabilia and artifacts to include in your heritage album fall into two categories.

• Paper memorabilia (ephemera): tickets, postcards, programs, labels, invitations, and announcements

• Artifacts: silverware, jewelry, furniture, souvenirs, hand-crafted items, and even houses

MAKING THOSE HEIRLOOMS TELL THEIR STORY

When you look for family history treasures in your attic, be sure to research the history behind the item so that you can better understand when it was popular and to whom it belonged.

Ask Questions

When you start to delve for data, don't forget to examine each artifact with these questions in mind:

• Are there any stories associated with it?

• Are there any photographs that include the object?

• What technical data is available in collector's guides and historical sources?

• What's the origin of the item, such as who owned it?

> **Heritage Album Tip:**
>
> *Anything too large to fit comfortably into a heritage album can be photographed and included that way.*

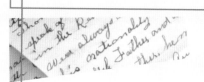

Library Research

Look for books and articles on similar objects or heirlooms so that you can learn when an item was popular, when it was made, and how it was used. You will also need to become familiar with the vocabulary specific to the type of item you are researching. Two useful resources are *Treasures in Your Attic* by Joe L. Rosson and Helaine Fendelman (Harper Resource, 2001) and *The Antiques Roadshow Primer* by Carol Prisant (Workman Publishing, 1999).

Online Sources

Using a standard search engine enter the type of item you have in the search box in quotation marks ("log cabin quilt," for example) and see what appears. You'll discover Web sites that link you to historical material or sites for collectors of certain types of items. Remember that a family artifact to you is a collectible to someone interested in antiques. The same types of sources they find useable will help you discover more about a particular artifact.

Collector Café

<www.collectorcafe.com>
Search this Web site for information on different types of collectibles.

Antiqnet.com

<www.antiqnet.com>
Post news on the message board or find a show or dealer in your area.

SKILL-BUILDING: DINNERWARE

The next time you sit down to eat, take a look at the plate your food is going to be served on. What do you know about your dinnerware? It might be more than a simple plate; it could be a connection to your family history. One day Nancy Smith's mother asked her to find out a little more about her dinnerware. Nancy knew her parents married in 1947 and that her mother bought the set in Macy's on a pre-wedding shopping trip to New York City with her mother. The dishes were what the young couple could afford at the time and were intended to be a "temporary" set of everyday dishes until a better set could be purchased. As so often happens, her parents used these dishes throughout their marriage and eventually gave them to Nancy along with a colorful yellow bowl. What a great story this is for Nancy's scrapbook.

Here's how she discovered more about her heirloom artifacts.

Ask Questions:
Don't forget to document the most important part of those dishes by asking family members about the history of the set through a series of questions:

When was it purchased?
Who owned it?
When was it used?

Trademarks:
Learning about your dishes is not difficult. There are a few definitions that help you understand your dinnerware. First, pattern refers to the decal in the center of the plate, while theme is the shape of the design around the edge. The markings on the back of the individual pieces are the trademark. By examining her mother's dishes, Nancy discovered they were made by Homer Laughlin.

To research your own dishes, start by turning over the item and examining the mark on the bottom. Try to find it in reference books on the company. Go online and see if you can find other material by typing the name of the company into a search engine. I found several Web sites by searching "Homer Laughlin."

Library Research:
Consulting books about Laughlin, Nancy found they were part of the Theme series in eggshell ivory. The mark on the bottom, K43N5, designated their origin in 1943. Theme, designed by Frederick Rhead, began production in 1939 with the characteristic raised fruit and flower design.

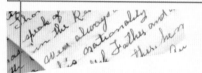

SKILL-BUILDING: DINNERWARE (CONTINUED)

During World War II, European china became unavailable, so Laughlin's wares increased in popularity. In 1941, a full thirty-two-piece set of Theme sold for a mere $4.98. Nancy's mother once owned a full set, complete with square luncheon plates, but Nancy only has one completely unblemished plate left while the rest of the dinner plates are cracked and worn.

She applied the same techniques to another bowl and it turned out to be valuable both as a collectible and as a family heirloom. It was made in Boston by the Saturday Evening Girls, a social experiment of the Arts and Crafts Movement that created opportunities for young immigrant women. A group of young Jewish and Italian immigrant women made these ceramics beginning in 1907 at the Paul Revere Pottery as part of a project founded by librarian Edith Guerrier and funded by philanthropist Helen Osborne Storrow. The Pottery was first located at 18 Hull Street in Boston's North End and eventually moved to Nottingham Hill in Brighton, Massachusetts, in 1915 where it remained until it ceased operation in 1969. The marks on the bottom of Nancy Smith's bowl are S.E.G. for the Saturday Evening Girls, the date of manufacture 12/14 (December 1914), and S.G. for Sara Galner, a well-known Arts and Crafts designer. On the inside is a saying, "O don't bother me said the Hen with

one chick" and the name Betsy. The name Betsy and the manufacturing date signify this as a birthday present for the one-year-old Elizabeth, Nancy's mother.

Consult Online Sources

• Homer Laughlin China Company Association ←www.hlcca.org→ Magazine and organization.

• *The Collector's Encyclopedia of Homer Laughlin China* by Joanne Jasper (Collector Books, 1993). A history of Laughlin China derived from Jasper's book is online at ←www.missing-piece.com/HLC_HISTORY.html→.

To find out more about the Saturday Evening Girls pottery, The Society for the Preservation of New

England Antiquities ←www.spnea.org→ has a short history on its Web site.

As with all family artifacts, you never know what you are going to discover. Write down your findings in a family history journal or create a scrapbook page of memories with history and pictures. What can you uncover about your family artifacts?

Heritage Album Tip:
Photocopy or scan a dinnerware pattern and use it as a decorative element in your scrapbook.

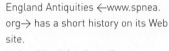

LOCATING MEMORABILIA AND ARTIFACTS

It's a rare person who doesn't have something that belonged to someone in the family. My sister has a button jar that belonged to my paternal grandmother. Gramma was not the type of person to waste anything, so any article of clothing too threadbare to be worn was stripped of its buttons and used as a cleaning rag. Funny thing about that button jar, some of the ones in the jar pre-dated my grandmother. I'm still tracking down information that places some of those buttons in a time frame, but I suspect that the person who began that jar was my great-grandmother. You might think you can't learn anything from a button, but a single one can tell you the type of garment it was worn on, who wore it–man, woman or child—and when it was made. You might even get lucky and find a photograph of someone wearing a garment with those buttons, and thereby tie them to an actual family member. So, now that you know even a lowly button can tell a story, take a look around your house and see what's old enough to have belonged to an earlier generation. There might even be a story in the family about a chair, spoon, or a dish.

Use an organized approach to what you have at home by going methodically from room to room (or box to box in the attic) and see what you have that once belonged to another family member. Examine everything from kitchen utensils to furniture to tools in the garage. You might uncover more than you expect. Unlike antique collectors, you are looking for items that have family history information, not necessarily monetary value. The pieces you locate might be battered and bruised from years of use or misuse, but that doesn't matter as long as you can discover who used it and when. Once you've looked around your own home, reach out to other family members.

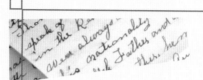

ITEMS TO LOOK FOR

- Ceramics and glass
- Clocks and watches
- Clothing
- Furniture
- Hand-crafted items (for example quilts, holiday ornaments, tablecloths, or toys)
- Jewelry
- Kitchen utensils
- Linens
- Metalwork
- Paper items (cards, invitations, and all sorts of ephemera)
- Needlework (quilts and samplers)
- Silver
- Tools
- Toys

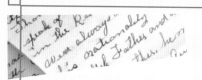

HOW TO EVALUATE SENTIMENTAL/ GENEALOGICAL VALUE VS. MARKET VALUE

In general, there are three questions you need to ask when determining the value of an item:

- Was it owned by a famous person?
- Is it unique?
- Is it in good condition?

If you want to sell one of your heirlooms, make sure you do your research first and have the item appraised. You can find an appraiser through:

- **American Society of Appraisers**
  ←www.appraisers.org→
  555 Herndon Parkway, Suite 125
  Herndon, VA 20170
  (703) 478-2228

- **Appraisers Association of America**
  ←www.appraisersassoc.org→
  386 Park Avenue South, Suite 2000
  New York, NY 10016
  (212) 889-5404

- **International Society of Appraisers**
  ←www.isa-appraisers.org→
  Riverview Plaza Office Park
  16040 Christensen Road, Suite 102
  Seattle, WA 98188-2929
  (206) 241-0359

ADDITIONAL RESOURCES

- *The Art of Family: Genealogical Artifacts in New England by D.* Brenton Simons and Peter Benes (NEHGS, 2002)

- *The Age of Homespun: Objects and Stories in the Creation of an American Myth* by Laurel Thatcher Ulrich (Knopf, 2001)

ASK RELATIVES

Do you know the provenance of the family artifact you own? Perhaps a relative knows the story of your grandmother's watch or someone else has a photograph of her wearing it. Even if you don't know anything about that mysterious chair in the corner of your living room, other relatives may know who owned it. Generally, items have an oral history as well as a written one. Probate documents that include inventories are one way to trace the history of ownership of an item.

Don't forget that relatives may also own family artifacts that you might want to include in your heritage album. You'll be able to include a photograph of the item in your album along with your relative's story about it.

If you've already contacted all the relatives you know, use online message boards to contact distant family and perhaps discover additional heirlooms that belonged to different ancestors.

Provenance: a list of the owners of an item. You can create a family tree for an artifact by discovering who owned it.

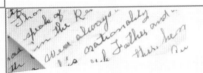

THE FUTURE OF YOUR MEMORABILIA, ARTIFACTS, AND HEIRLOOMS

- **Make a will**

A special consideration for your family collections is to pass this heritage on to other family members through a will. This insures that your wishes will be carried out and that your artifacts will go to the family member you specify instead of in an estate sale.

- **Donate**

Should you decide to donate memorabilia and artifacts to a special library or museum, contact them now to find out about their gift procedures. They may not be interested and can suggest another, more appropriate repository.

- **Insure a valuable item**

Get information and an estimate from your homeowners insurance company on insuring family heirlooms.

SEARCH PRIVATE COLLECTIONS

If you know where generations of your ancestors lived, contact the local museum or historical society to see if they own any items that belonged to your family. You might be able to order photographs of the item or visit and photograph it yourself. Policies vary by institution.

AUCTIONS

To locate auctions in your area, use an online search engine and type in "antique auction." Scroll down the listings until you find one or you could consult a couple of publications such as:

Maine Antique Digest
<www.maineantiquedigest.com>
911 Main St.
PO Box 1429
Waldoboro, ME 04572
(207) 832-7534

Look in your local phone book for antique dealers in your area and pick up the free papers available in most shops. These contain local listings and show schedules.

Auction Web Sites

• eBay.com
This site is practically a household name, with listings on just about every conceivable object or item. Consult tips for users before looking for ancestral memorabilia.

• Pastconnect.com
<www.pastconnect.com>
Bid on historical memorabilia.

• Antique Collectors Club
<www.antiquecc.com>
Search either the United States or United Kingdom catalogs for items.

Reunion Web Sites

• Ancestors Lost and Found
<www.usgennet.org/usa/topic/ancestors/>
Post a listing for a "lost treasure" or search the list of items individuals are willing to share.

RESOURCES: CARING FOR MEMORABILIA AND ARTIFACTS

Your approach to caring for the material in your family depends on what it is. Paper ephemera items require storage conditions similar to photographs and documents (see Chapters 2 and 3), while clothing and furniture need other types of containers and care. Before you attempt to clean and store these items for the future consult these two guides:

• *Caring for Your Collections* edited by Arthur W. Schultz (Harry Abrams, 1992)

• *Caring For Your Family Treasures* by Jane S. and Richard W. Long (Harry Abrams, 2000)

Of course, if any item is in need of restoration or conservation, the basic rule is to contact a professional conservator through the American Institute for Conservation of Historic and Artistic Works <aic.stanford.edu>, 1717 K Street NW, Suite 200, Washington, DC 20006, (202) 452-9545. The AIC can send you a list of conservators who specialize in the

type of material that needs conservation. Never attempt this type of work yourself because you could end up destroying the future value of the artifacts. Professional conservators are trained to care for museum-quality artifacts and received advanced training in an area of specialty.

USING HEIRLOOMS, MEMORABILIA, AND ARTIFACTS IN A SCRAPBOOK

There are so many ways to incorporate heirlooms, memorabilia, and artifacts in your heritage album. Here are three ideas. See Chapter 7 for additional suggestions.

• Create Mylar sleeves or buy premade polypropylene envelopes for fragile paper items.

• Use hard plastic storage boxes (available in a variety of shapes and sizes) for items that can't be stored flat.

• Take photographs of heirlooms in other family members' collections.

my COAT of many (green) COLORS

Great Grandma Frost was always sewing, crocheting or quilting something for her grandchildren. One of the wonderful things I received is this very 1970's crazy quilted jacket. Grandma Frost made a red one for my sister Jenny and a blue one for Becky, and gave them to us for our birthdays in 1978.

This photo shows four generations: Grandma Evelyn Lucille Frost Seeger (who continues the hand-crafting tradition) with me, Diane Frances Haddad, age 1. Mom Mary Christine Seeger Haddad is holding my sister, Rebecca Marie. Great Grandma Alvina Philomena Thoss Frost has my sister Jennifer Lyn, age 4. Photo taken 1975.

Title lettering template: Journaling Genie by Chatterbox. Tip: Bring acid lignin-free paper with you to a copy center, and use a color copy as a background paper.

—Diane Haddad

CHAPTER FIVE

MAKING YOUR ANCESTOR A REAL PERSON

T elling the story of your ancestors is about more than names and dates; it's making them come alive by placing them in history. After all, our lives are affected every day by world and local events that influence our decisions just as our ancestors' were. So, how can you discover what you need to know about their daily habits, activities, and the news events that changed their lives? Through consulting family members, doing library research, and locating online resources, you'll discover what the world was like when your ancestors were alive. What you'll be doing is investigating social history.

QUESTIONS TO ANSWER

Food:

What did they eat?

Consult old cookbooks or magazines for recipes.

Clothing:

What did they wear?

Until recently, most individuals had a limited wardrobe consisting of work and church clothes. Costume encyclopedias available through your public library provide you with a general sense of typical attire. You might not be familiar with some of the fabrics mentioned, such as towcloth—an inexpensive colonial cloth made from flax—but a dictionary can unravel those mysteries.

Occupations:

What did they do for work?

City directories and census documents list occupations, but consult a special dictionary (see the list on page 79) for terms you don't understand.

Health:

Were they healthy?

Death records will tell you the cause of death but won't specify other non-fatal illnesses. Learn about epidemics and other more common illnesses by studying the history of the time.

Look for items around your house that will make your ancestor come alive. Work badge, General Electric. Collection of the author.

You've already done some of this research by dating old photographs, looking at documents, and researching memorabilia, but now it's time to put all that history together in a single context—the times in which they lived. Brush off those schoolhouse tools for writing a history paper and locate sources that can help you try to understand your ancestors.

ASK QUESTIONS

Do you know why a group of ancestors kept moving from place to place? I suspect some of mine moved in front of the rent collector, but then again, adding up the clues and putting together the elements of social history might uncover other reasons. One ancestor disabled during the Civil War kept moving to find employment to feed his growing family.

Leave nothing out of your consideration. Even the weather affects our lives today. That's part of the reason it appears in so many diaries! Harsh conditions, epidemics, and economic downturns left lasting scars on our families. Now it's time to add a little historical perspective to the facts, images, and things you've collected.

Library at the New England Historic Genealogical Society, 101 Newbury St., Boston, MA 02116. New England Historic Genealogical Society.

SKILL-BUILDING: WORKING WITH REFERENCE STAFF

Reference librarians are trained to conduct a reference interview with each patron to help them identify materials in their holdings that can help answer the patron's question. Getting a question answered is a matter of knowing how to ask one.

• Ask a specific question, but don't tell them your family history.
• Be organized.
• Ask what online resources are available for in-library use and if any can be used from home.

SKILL-BUILDING: TIMELINES

Create a timeline of history and your ancestor's life.

Draw a line and place all the events in your ancestor's life on one side and world or local events on the other. There are also computer programs that help you create timelines such as Genelines (Progeny Software) ←www.progeny.com→.

If you are looking for locality-specific timelines, see ←www.cyndis list.com→ under "Timelines."

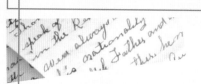

INTERLIBRARY LOAN

One of the wonders of the Internet is the ability to search card catalogs for libraries all over the world. You're probably wondering what good that does you. Well, welcome to the inter-library loan. Public libraries can order copies of books and magazine articles from other libraries for you to use. Ask your local library about its policies. There may be a charge for this service.

TECHNIQUES TO FOLLOW YOUR ANCESTORS IN HISTORY

Visit the reference section of your public library.

Even the smallest public library has a reference set of books that fall into categories that can be enormously helpful. Listed below are just a few of the publications that help place your ancestors in historical context. Your local public reference librarian can assist you in identifying helpful books in your own library.

General Encyclopedias

This category includes those multi-volume sets you are probably familiar with, as well as those that are more specific in nature.

- *Britannica*

  A standard reference source is Britannica because it offers in-depth information on topics. It has two indexes: macropedia and micropedia. Today you can even search this set online at <www.britannica.com>.

- *Encyclopedia of Native American Tribes* edited by Sharon Malinowski (Gale, 1998)

  If you know you have Native American ancestry, use this reference source to learn more about tribal culture and history.

- *Harvard Encyclopedia of American Ethnic Groups* edited by Stephan Thernstrom (Belknap Press, Harvard University, 1980)

  A classic for anyone who needs background information on when and why their ancestors immigrated to the United States.

Biographical Encylopedias

Did one of your ancestors do something noteworthy? You might be surprised to find them listed in an old edition of *Who's Who* or find them mentioned in a nineteenth-century county history or "mug book," so named because individuals wrote their own biography, included a picture of themselves, and sometimes paid for the entry.

Since 1899, *Marquis Who's Who in America* has been the leading publisher of annual biographical volumes on prominent individuals. An online database is available as a subscription service to libraries.

Ancestry.com offers its subscribers access to a variety of biographical sources. Subscribe to Ancestry's free online newsletter "The Daily News" to keep up with new databases added daily to the site.

Chronologies

If you want to set your ancestors in the time period in which they lived, you'll need to know world events that affected their lives. There are a number of timeline books and online sites to help you do that.

- *Chronicle of the World* edited by Jerome Burne (DK, 1996)

- *American Eras* (Gale, 1997-) This eight-volume set covers different periods of American History from 1600-1899.

- *American Decades* (Gale, 1996-2001) Ten volumes cover each decade of the twentieth century 1900-1999. Also available on CD-ROM.

- *20th Century Day by Day* (DK, 2000) A daily account of what happened in the world in the twentieth century.

*Taylor Family.
Collection of
the author.*

Dictionaries

A good dictionary is a valuable resource. Everyone should either own one or have access to one through a library. While standard dictionaries are helpful, the premier source of information on the English language is the *Oxford English Dictionary*, 20 vols., (Clarendon Press, 1989). This multi-volume wonder tells you the history of a word and how it was used. That means you'll be able to see how your ancestor used an unfamiliar phrase in an old document and what it meant.

Other special dictionaries are also part of a family historian's basic toolbox such as *A-Zax: A Comprehensive Dictionary for Genealogists & Historians* by Barbara Jean Evans (Hearthside, 1995). Want to know more about an ancestor's occupation, cause of death, or the definition of a weird word? This tiny volume will probably help you fill in the gap.

Historical Newspapers and Magazines

Reading newspapers and magazines lets you experience history as it was printed. It's now easier than ever to find them on microfilm using inter-library loan or online through sub-scription databases such as Ancestry.com and Accessible Archives.com.

Magazines and Journals

History, archaeology, and antiques magazines can help you in surpris-ing ways. For instance, because of the lack of newspapers and maga-zines in early Colonial New England, you'll have to turn to contemporary magazines for stories and research in order to learn about your ancestors' daily lives. There is a magazine for just about every interest. Amazon.com offers magazine sub-scriptions that you can search by subject. Most of the titles of interest to family historians are in the catego-ry "History."

A useful tool for locating appropri-ate articles is the periodical database Infotrac, subscribed to by many pub-lic and academic libraries. You can search it by subject, keyword, or spe-cific journal. This is just one of the reference tools that can help you with your genealogical research. Find out about special databases and online search tools that your library offers by asking the reference staff.

Postcard of Peru, Vermont Collection of the author.

LEARN MORE ABOUT DAILY LIFE

In order to bring your ancestors back to life in the pages in your heritage album, you'll want to read about how people in those time periods lived and worked. Thankfully, there are a few sets of books that help writers, historians, and you do that.

Books
• *Writer's Digest Everyday Life Series* Consult a series of books that writers use to set their characters into a time frame. These books are full of the details you'll need to bring your ancestors back to life. Consult the Writer's Digest Web site for a current list of titles <www.writersdigest.com>

• *Everyday Life in America Series* Published by Harper Perennial, there are several books in the series that tell you how your ancestors really lived. Each book in the series is written by a historian.

• *As Various as Their Land: The Everyday Lives of Eighteenth-Century Americans* by Stephanie Grauman Wolf (Harper Perennial, 1993)

• *Everyday Life in Early America* by David Freeman Hawke (Harper Collins, 1989)

• *Victorian America: Transformations in Everyday Life, 1876-1915* by Thomas J. Schlereth (Harper Perennial, 1992)

• *The Expansion of Everyday Life, 1860-1876* by Daniel E. Sutherland (University of Arkansas Press, 2000)

• *The Reshaping of Everyday Life, 1790-1840* by Jack Larkin (Harper Perennial, 1989)

• *The Uncertainty of Everyday Life, 1915-1945* by Harvey Green (University of Arkansas Press, 2000)

HOMETOWN HISTORY

Breathe life into your ancestors by setting them in the context of their hometown. It's easy.

• Begin by finding out if the public library system in that area has an online card catalog and search for historical materials in its holdings or try the online card catalog of the country's largest library, the Library of Congress <www.loc.gov>, for relevant publications. If you are unable to locate these materials in your area, chances are your public library can borrow books or order copies of articles through its interlibrary loan program. If there is no single volume on the town you're interested in, try looking at county histories. Even small villages rate a notation in some of these late nineteenth-century compilations.

• If you want to purchase books, try using online booksellers such as Amazon.com and BarnesandNoble.com or vendors that specialize in local material. For instance, Cyndi's List <www.cyndislist.com> mentions publishers under locality categories. If you visit those hometowns, don't forget to browse bookstores (used and new) in the area. Most have a local history section and you'll be able to make purchases after perusing the selections. Also check out the Web site of <www.Arcadiapublishing.com>, which publishes pictorial histories of many towns and neighborhoods throughout the country.

• The Periodical Source Index (PERSI) online or on CD-ROM is one way to locate articles on a particular town. It is an index of genealogical and local history periodicals in the United States and Canada since 1800. Search by surname or locality and then order copies of the articles either through the interlibrary loan program in your town or directly from the Allen County Public Library. Use the directions on the Ancestry.com Web site at <www.ancestry.com/search/rectype/periodicals/persi/about.htm> and follow instructions for making requests. In addition, your public library might have online indexes for searching periodicals. You'll be surprised at what you can uncover using standard resources available in most public libraries.

• Consult contemporary and historical travel guides to learn about the important or interesting sites in the areas and during the time periods your ancestors lived there. For instance, Cambridge, Massachusetts, publisher Moses King printed a series of travel guides for late nineteenth-century tourists on a variety of cities. They are full of pictures and information on landmarks and everyday life. You can locate similar guides through library card catalogs.

BECOME YOUR ANCESTOR FOR A DAY

Whether you take a trip to a living history museum, sleep in a historic inn, or participate in a re-enactment, you'll get a better sense of what your ancestors' lives were like. The whole experience will leave you wanting to know more and put you in the mood to create those heritage pages. A state-by-state listing of those events or places appeared in *Heritage Travel* magazine (May 2002). Visit <www.familytree magazine.com> to order your copy.

Now that you know how to bring your ancestor back to life, turn what you've learned into a creative set of heritage album pages. Each one will be an interesting history lesson in itself. Even if your kids or relatives aren't the least bit interested in history, seeing what you've discovered and created is bound to change their minds.

CHAPTER SIX

TELLING THE STORY

N ow that you know who your ancestors and relatives are, the challenge is to create heritage pages that present your research in an easy-to-understand graphic layout. Basics such as captions, labels, or journal entries for each item or photograph need to be included as ways to tell the story of your family. You decide the format, the design, and layout, but the basic rule is to include enough information so that anyone can understand the story. Sound easy? It is if you use the following techniques and tools.

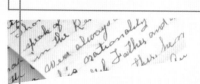

TO MAKE PULL-OUT JOURNALING

• Mark photo placement on background sheet.

• Cut and glue a "holder" for the journaling plaque from a plastic page protector.

• Attach with double stick tape to background paper where it will be concealed by the photo.

• Cut journaling plaque to fit inside holder and protrude from top.

• Journal and insert in holder.

• Affix photo over holder using photo mounting tape.

• Place page in page protector, slit protector where plaque emerges from behind photo.

   This page title: Design and print it out on a computer. Scribble with a pencil on the back to make homemade carbon paper. Place pencil side down on title background. Trace letters with pencils to transfer pattern. (paper: Frances Meyer)

—Diane Haddad

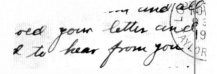

CAPTIONING TECHNIQUES

The key to having viewers of your scrapbook family history understand the images and artifacts depends on the layout and the way you identify them. Captions can take several forms. It doesn't matter whether you use bulleted highlights or poetic expressions, just remember to label everything and leave room for journaling.

Labeling

Labeling is a way to provide identifying information for the photographs or items in your scrapbook. Museum curators include the basics: full name, life dates, and date and place taken (if known). For instance: Esther Jean (Smith) Weeks (1892-1968), 1961, on her seventieth birthday. In this case both her first and middle names are known; the name in parentheses is her maiden name; followed by her married name, life dates; and year and occasion for the image. Labels are a simple way to identify the basics in order to use more pictures to tell the story of a single event or to include more people and captions on the page. You should label every picture so that people viewing the album know who is in each image, but this can also be done with journaling.

Journaling

Another useful tool is to tell the story of the image in a journal format. Do

this by writing your memories of particular items or events or let relatives tell a story in their own words. This can be an effective way to relate all the details in a particular photograph or set of images. This can be done by telling a single story or using a diary format (ideal for vacation photographs), in which you tell the events of a specific period of time day-by-day in words and pictures.

Biography

Another way to journal your scrapbook is to write the biography of the person you are representing in images, artifacts, and documents. Augment the vital statistics of your ancestor's life with the social history of the time period in which he lived.

Memoir

Memoirs are a very personal form of journaling. They are a description of your memories of the person on your family tree. Be sure to use labels to include the basic facts of the person's life.

Alvina Philomina Theiss
wed
Edward George Frost
July 4, 1925

St. Benedict Church
Covington, Kentucky

Great Grandma & Grandpa Frost
Pressed flowers from Alvina's bouquet

Choose beautiful background paper so you don't need to add extra embellishments. Use a wide solid mat to separate the photo from the pattern. Place flowers in plastic pockets so that they don't come in contact with the photograph or fall apart. (paper: Anna Griffin)

—Diane Haddad

RECORDING YOUR SOURCES

Artistic presentations don't lend themselves to footnotes, but genealogists like to be able to go back to original records, so try to include essential source information so that others can re-create your research or get more information. You might think, "why bother?" But suppose you suddenly needed to retrace your research steps to prove a new branch on your family tree. If you couldn't find the source for a piece of information, you might have to look at an assortment of records before you stumble upon the right one. Don't leave anything to chance. Place a note in your heritage album about where you found your information. Generations of family historians will thank you!

Resource

Make sure you format all those references right the first time by consulting *The Sleuth Book for Genealogists: Strategies for More Successful Family History Research* by Emily Anne Croom (Betterway Books, 2000).

Resources:
• *The Photo Scribe: A Writing Guide: How to Write the Stories Behind Your Photographs* by Denis Ledoux (Soleil Press, 1998)

• *Scrapbook Storytelling* by Joanna Campbell-Slan (Betterway Books, 1999)

• *Scrapbook Journaling Made Simple* (Memory Makers, 2002)

FAMILY STORIES TO TELL

• The story of your ancestor's immigration journey with information on traveling conditions, a passenger list, a photograph of the ship, and a map tracing their route.

• An ancestor portrayed with pictures, her favorite sayings, images of things she owned or made, and an autograph.

• Childhood memories of an ancestor with historical information on a child's life at that point in history.

• Weddings in the family, complete with pictures, wedding history, and clippings.

• The history of your family's involvement with a town or a particular building such as the village church or town school.

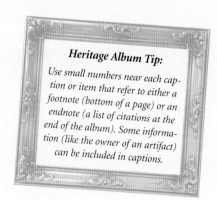

Heritage Album Tip:

Use small numbers near each caption or item that refer to either a footnote (bottom of a page) or an endnote (a list of citations at the end of the album). Some information (like the owner of an artifact) can be included in captions.

Isaac Collins Family Tree, New England Historic Genealogical Society.

"A Genealogical Family Piece," Dodge Family, 1809 New England Historic Genealogical Society.

CHARTS

The ways genealogists have represented family relationships have changed over time. In the Middle Ages, genealogy charts were hand-drawn and documented complicated royal intermarriages. In the eighteenth century, young girls painted family trees adorned with apples and hearts containing the names of relatives, or they stitched names in needlework samplers. By the late nineteenth century, family historians commissioned engravings of trees to hold the names of their ancestors and included certain icons to convey a sense of family history. With the advent of computer programs in the twentieth century, anyone can create a variety of charts by inputing data into a software program. You can also purchase pre-printed charts to add to your heritage album. The fact is, there are more choices than ever before to help you organize and tell your family history. The choice is yours.

There are standard charts that genealogists use such as the pedigree chart explained in Chapter 1 or the standard fan chart. Computer software programs offer other options. See Chapter 10 for a list of programs. Here is a list of the most popular types of trees.

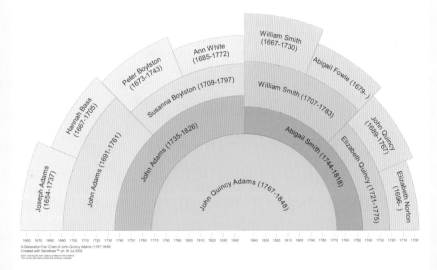

Fan Chart created with Genelines (Progeny Software).

Ancestor Trees
These trees show a person's ancestors. You can choose from a variety of formats.

Traditional trees
Similar to a pedigree chart because ancestors branch off from the starting individual. You can select whether your tree is vertical or horizontal.

Fan Chart
The first person is in the center in a circle with ancestors going in all directions. There are also half-fan charts for either maternal or paternal lines. At a glance, you'll be able to see who is missing from your family tree.

All-in-one Tree
Includes everyone in your family: ancestors, descendants, and cousins. Family Tree Maker software offers this tree as part of its chart options. This format works well with small family groups; it's too confusing for larger families.

Heritage Album Tip:
As you share your heritage album with family, carry along multiple copies of your page layout and see if anyone has information on the missing links.

Descendant Trees
Instead of focusing on yourself as the first person in a tree, begin with your immigrant ancestor and bring forward that person's descendants using either a fan chart or a traditional tree like the historical examples shown earlier.

Hourglass Tree
You appear in the middle with parents and grandchildren listed below and ancestors above. This tree shows both ancestors and descendants in an easy-to-understand format.

Heritage Album Tip:
Use your creative efforts to duplicate the look of the historical examples shown in this chapter. It is also possible to purchase pre-printed family records that resemble ones used in the past.

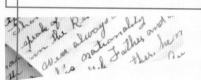

Basic Tips to Remember

- Use a simple design.
- Don't overload your page with too many patterns, die cuts, and designs.
- Use photographs, documents, and keepsakes sparingly.

The idea behind a scrapbook is to tell a story so that anyone can understand it, not to use everything you've collected. You can always create another album or add a page to the book you've compiled.

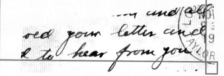

Heritage Album Tip:

Use a computer-generated chart as a template and make your own creative presentation of the information.

Outline Descendant Tree

This looks more like a traditional outline, with each generation indented to the right. This could appear as a table of contents or an index for your heritage album.

Waterfall Chart

According to *Family Tree Magazine* contributing editor Rick Crume in his article "The ABC's of Charts and Reports" (June 2002), a waterfall chart shows descendants cascading down from the upper left to lower right.

NON–TRADITIONAL FAMILIES

There are graphic ways to design charts and pages for families that don't fit the traditional nuclear family. Let's face it: families have always been diverse.

Adoption Chart

The standard format for adoptive families is to use a two-way chart or tree that features the adoptee in the center with birth family on one side and adoptive family on the other.

There are other creative ways of dealing with non-traditional families and they all involve stepping away from the traditional tree format. Use your imagination to think of other ways to represent your family. Children can come up with the most creative solutions, such as using a pile of leaves (the children are on top and grandparents on the bottom) or boats on a lake. One child even included deceased relatives as clouds in the sky over a family scene.

for Evelyn Lucille Frost (my Grandmother), August 1946. Because of shortages after World War II, ladies held tin can teas instead of showers for brides-to-be. Rather than china and silverware, brides received tin cans full of food. Grandma married Grandpa Richard Alvin Seeger on September 25, 1946.

Above, left to right:
Great Great Aunt Lily (Norris) O'Neal
Great Great Aunt Mayme Seeger
Great Grandma Mayme (Norris) Seeger
Great Grandma Alvina (Thoss) Frost
Great Aunt Lorraine Seeger
Great Great Grandma Celestine (Koop) Thoss

PUTTING IT ALL TOGETHER

Heritage albums are complex because of the combination of family history storytelling, pictures, and design. As you select the type of chart, format for sources, and design elements, you'll want to keep in mind the story you are trying to tell. You probably learned about outlining from a school English teacher. While you don't need to follow a formal outline, making a list of individuals or topics to include in your scrapbook with a subhead of items you've collected on each will keep you organized and focused. Don't worry about using every single fact, document, picture, or artifact. You can file those away or use them in another type of page. Planning is one of the most important phases of creating a scrapbook. Many professions use graphic organizers to help them plan, so apply the same technique to a single page or an album. Sketch on a piece of paper a preliminary layout of what you'd like each page to look like. Use a system to layout your page and album that works for you. Some scrapbookers like to use drawings while others just jump in and layout the materials on the page trying different formats. Whether you use a formal outline or a thumbnail graphic layout for planning your family history album, it will be the first step towards actually pulling together your heritage album.

CHAPTER SEVEN

WORKING WITH A THEME

The goal of a heritage album is to tell the story of your family. You decide the focus by including a single person or a whole family. It can be the story of one person's military service, the way your family immigrated to this country, a romantic tale of a family wedding, or even the story of your ancestor's place in a small town. In Sharon DeBartolo Carmack's *Your Guide to Cemetery Research* (Betterway Books, 2002), she discusses creating a cemetery scrapbook. You've worked hard to collect the materials you need to tell your tale. Now it's time to put it all together.

FINDING A THEME

Sometimes the collection of objects, photographs, and documents dictates a theme. For instance, you might have a group of material about an ancestor's military experiences or a wedding. Let the materials help you organize your book and pages.

Whether you tell the story of one individual, family, or an event, it is still a heritage album if you've incorporated family history techniques. Most published genealogies start with the immigrant ancestor and continue to the present. Part of organizing your heritage album is thinking about chronology. You can either go forward or backwards in time, the choice is yours. See Chapter 6 for some additional ideas.

Collage of different military-themed items. Paper (Frances Meyer, Inc.); Paperkins (EK Success); album (K & Co.).

Actually laying out the page is one of the scariest parts of scrapbooking, so think about the following details when picking a theme. Consider organizing your album according to branches on your family tree such as your father and mother, maternal and paternal grandparents, or just one person and his siblings. As you plan your heritage album you'll also need to ask yourself these questions:

Heritage Album Tip:

Decide on a focus: events, person, or whole family.

• Do you have enough material to create a page? If not, fill in with journaling, clipart, and newspaper or magazine clippings.

• Who will you include in your album?

• Will you focus on couples, individuals, or extended family?

• What type of chronological arrangement will you use?

• What type of charts will you use to help guide viewers through the album? (See the list in Chapter 6.)

• What design elements will you use to convey a different feeling for each time period?

There are three basic steps to creating a scrapbook after you decide on a focus.

• Set up a clean work area that you can use to lay out your collections and store your materials. Be sure to wash your hands and wear clean cotton gloves before handling originals. This will protect them from any dirt or oils that might be present on your hands.

• Purchase materials. Be sure to use only archival materials to create your album. (See suggestions in Chapter 9.)

• Lay out the items. Deciding what to include in your album can be a daunting task when faced with boxes and notebooks full of materials. Choose items that relate to your theme and are good quality. You can always create another heritage album with a different theme.

SELECTING PHOTOGRAPHS, ARTIFACTS, AND DOCUMENTS

Photographs

• Select images that are in focus.

• If you're cropping or gluing pictures, never use original heritage photographs; use copies. Once you've cut a heritage photograph, you've destroyed it for future generations.

• Encapsulate or de-acidify before placing in an album.

Artifacts

• If an artifact is too big to include, use a photograph or photocopy of it, incorporate the elements in your design, or scan a section of it.

• To display smaller items, use plastic sleeves made expressly for them, such as those produced by Fiskars.

Documents

• Make sure the handwriting is legible; otherwise, transcribe the document or use only the author's signiture

• Encapsulate or de-acidify before placing in an album.

• Rather than include whole documents, transcribe the important sections. Using too many documents clutters the page. File the originals using the methods described in Chapter 9.

COPYING TECHNIQUES

Photographic Copies

• Use a digital camera to make a copy with a steady hand or a tripod; you can take digital images of heritage photographs.

• When you take film to be developed, order an extra set of prints or a CD (to make copies at home).

The addition of a narrow cream colored photo mat lightens the browns on this page and reflects the color of the journaling plaque. (embossed vellum–K & Co.)–Diane Haddad.

• Make a copy using a self-operated machine such as Kodak's Picture Maker. It allows you to crop, enlarge, reduce red-eye, and add creative borders. You can make prints that range from wallet size to eight-by-twelve-inches or download the picture to a disk.

Scanning

With scanners available for less than one hundred dollars, there is no reason not to own one. Most come with editing software and some that lead you through the process. You can scan photographs, memorabilia, and even small artifacts. The abbreviations are a little confusing at first, so here's a guide:

DPI: Dots per inch. More dots per inch means a higher resolution and a better image. The higher the resolution, the more storage space an image will occupy on your computer.

TIFF: An uncompressed file format

viewable on both a PC and a Macintosh.

PICT: A file type for images only used on a Macintosh.

GIF: A file type used on the Web. Images are compressed to save file space and are limited in color. GIFs are compatible with PCs and Macs.

JPEG: Another file type used on the Web. Images are compressed to save file space and are compatible with either computer format.

Heritage Album Tip:

Keep it simple. Generally heritage albums look best with few embellishments because it keeps the look of your pages timeless. Using trendy scrapbook supplies tends to date an album.

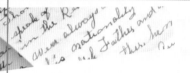

IMPROVING THE QUALITY OF DAMAGED IMAGES

- **Photo-editing Software**

  The editing program that comes with your scanner will let you improve an image by lightening the picture or removing flaws such as cracks or red-eye. The process of fixing or repairing an image using a computer is called digital restoration.

- **Airbrushing**

  Hire a professional restoration expert to use a pressurized paint-brush to add pigment to a photo-graphic copy print.

- **Photographic Enhancement**

  A professional photographer using special film, filters, and chemistry can enhance a faded image.

Restoration plus sepia toned print. The only original this person had was a fourth genera-tion copy print. A fourth generation copy print is a copy made from a copy made from a copy made from the original. David Mishkin—Just Black & White.

A GUIDE TO VINTAGE FABRICS:

with assistance from Marianne Schwers of Vintage and Vogue

1800	1830	1860	1890	1920	1950	1980

1810-40
Blue, white, chartruse, pinks, reds, tan, beige, brown, yellow, green, and black.

1830-60
Brown, brownish red, pinks, prussian blue, purples, and turkey red.

1840-60s
Prussian blue (1835-1850), turkey red, poison green, chrome yellow, chrome orange, and bright plaids (1840s-1950s).

1850s-60s
Lancaster blue.

1860s
Mint green with white; turkey red, indigo, chrome yellow, double pinks, and robin blue.

1870s and 1880s
Browns; chocolate brown, London brown, cocoa brown, madder brown, madder red, double pinks, double purples, double yellows, double blues, Perkins purple, Hamilton blue, robin's egg blue, black, Cadet blue, red, turkey red, grays, blacks. (After this period browns don't return to any significant degree until the 1970s.)

1890-1910
Burgundy or wine red, navy, indigo with chrome orange, indigo with red, "true black," tan, black with true red, pink, light blue, mourning prints (black with white almost creates a charcoal appearance), almost NO brown, greys, silvers, various shades of light blue, Garibaldi prints; (1890s), stripes, shirtings.

1930s
Nile green, Copen blue, butter yellow, daffodil yellow, lilac, lavender, true red, white, orange, tangerine, true red, rose pink, and pale pink.

1940s
Add to 1930s colors more red, larger scale prints, navy, red and white, black and white, and brighter pinks.

1950s
Military colors: navy, khaki, olive green, and yellow as well as deep greens, turquoise and kingfisher blue, black, turquoise, pink, black and white, coral, and red.

1950s-60s
Cowboy prints and rocket and outer space motifs.

As you scan images, you'll be asked to select output type (200 dpi works for most items), resolution (low, medium, or high) and type of image. For type of image, choose color when you want to reproduce the original look of a heritage photograph or make it a black and white image.

SETTING YOUR PAGE IN THE TIME PERIOD

Color Choices

With today's computer programs offering more than a couple hundred color choices, it is easy to assume that most of those colors have always been around. However, colors were created from natural sources until 1856 when William H. Perkin, an English chemist, created mauve (pale purple). This accidental discovery created a demand for new colors.

Using period colors in your heritage album can place the photographs and other articles in the context of the times. Most colors only remain in fashion for approximately a decade. Use papers and inks to accent or create a historic look for your album. If you are looking for colors specific to the period in which your ancestor lived, you have a variety of options:

• Consult the color wheels in the heritage album issue of *Memory Makers* magazine (Fall 2001).

• Look at advertisements from the time period to see what the popular colors were, then try to find paper that approximates the look.

• View historic fabric colors such as those used in quilts or old clothing to develop a sense of the shades used in each decade.

• Good aesthetic color choices for backgrounds for sepia-toned photographs are burgundy, navy, parchment, and brown.

• Use period colors as an accent if the images don't look good against the background.

• Keep in mind that heritage photographs come in a wide variety of colors that can be accented with certain paper colors such as dark blue, cream, and burgundy.

Period Colors

For a reference guide to fabric colors with illustrations, consult quilting books such as *America's Glorious Quilts* edited by Dennis Duke and Deborah Harding (Macmillan, 1987).

Resources

• Vintage & Vogue
P.O. BOX 786
Hollis, NH 03049
<www.vintageandvogue.com>

They offer a selection of one hundred percent cotton fabrics from 1750 to 2000, many of which are reproductions of museum collections.

• Sally Queen Associates
2801 S. Joyce Street
Arlington, VA 22202
(888) 266-7298
<www.sallyqueenassociates.com>

Sells three books on historic clothing and fabrics. This site has great links to books and articles.

WAYS TO ADD INTEREST TO YOUR THEME

Albums

You can purchase albums that allow you to focus on a theme. Some come with cut-outs on the front cover for a photograph and a title. If you don't want to leave future generations guessing, include your name and the date you created the album. Albums also come in different sizes. It doesn't matter what size you use, as long as you purchase it before you buy other sup-

plies. Smaller albums are easier to carry around, but larger pages enable you to include more details and journaling.

Stamps and Inks

Stamps are available in a variety of vintage designs or have your own stamps made through stationery stores. Use inks in the period colors for stamping, journaling, or design elements.

Stickers

Some companies now offer reproductions of Victorian scrap or stickers of artifacts, clothing, and other items used in different decades.

Borders and Frames

Make your own borders and frames using designs present in some of the artifacts collected. Purchase laser cuts that mimic the border styles present in period advertisements or make your own by tracing or photocopying them. Use patterned paper for attractive edging or use border paper punches to add interest.

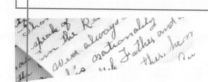

OTHER TYPES OF ITEMS IN YOUR ALBUM

As long as you use copy photographs and documents in your heritage album, you can use newer materials in your heritage album. These materials will shorten the life-span of your album, but as long as they don't come in contact with original heritage photographs they are safe. For more tips on creating an album that will last generations, consult Chapter 8. Here are a few words of caution:

Fibers, fabrics, yarn, embroidery floss:

Make sure the product is color-fast. If the dye bleeds in water, don't use it.

Eyelets and other metals:

If your album is exposed to high humidity or water, the metal may rust and damage the rest of your album.

Shrinky Dinks, clay, crayon, glitter:

Unless these items are photo-safe, don't use them. If you want to include a child's drawing in your album, hand her a pencil or marker considered safe for use in scrapbooks. The wax in crayons is affected by heat and the color can transfer to your pages.

Natural materials:

Include plants, rocks, and other natural items in plastic sleeves to protect the rest of your page from their deterioration or abrasiveness.

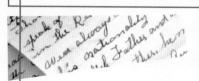

SKILL-BUILDING: CLIP ART

Enliven your pages with clip art from books, CD-ROMs, or the Internet. Try these sources or search for "clip art" in online search engines.

Web Sites

- **Miss Mary's Victorian Clip-Art**
  ←www.victorianlinks.com/clip_art/index.shtml→
  Subscribe to her free newsletter, print clip-art, or find new sites through links.
- **Kat's Victorian Clip-Art Collection**
  ←www.geocities.com/Heartland/Valley/6773/vicgifs.html→
  With images taken from postcards, greeting cards, and other Victorian paper sources, this site features a color bar to show you what the clippings look like on different backgrounds.

Publications

- **Dover Publications**
  ← store.doverpublications.com→
  Order a free catalog:
  Dover Publications
  Customer Care Department
  31 East 2nd Street
  Mineola, NY 11501-3852

CD-ROMs

- **Old Time Clip Art**
  ←www.oldtimeclipart.com→
  Use a limited amount of art from the site or order the collection on CD.
- **Dover Deskgallery Mega-bundle**
  (Dover, 1996)

SKILL-BUILDING: RECREATE OLD HANDWRITING OR TYPEFACES

There are quite a few different lettering and fonts available on CD-ROM, but you can also trace lettering from old handwriting manuals, period magazines, and newspapers. If you want to duplicate these styles by hand, consult Patricia Lovett's *Calligraphy & Illumination: A History and Practical Guide* (Harry Abrams, 2000) with its detailed instructions and interesting history of manuscript illumination.

- See the handwriting samples in Chapter 3 for handwriting styles popular in particular time periods.
- Look at magazine covers, posters, and advertisements from the time period you are trying to re-create.

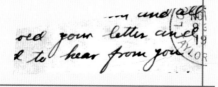

More Ideas

Add patterns to your pages to re-create the time period in which your ancestor lived.

- Use designs found on ancestral artifacts.
- Stencil or cross stitch designs.
- Sew a pattern on the paper or use cloth pages.
- Crochet an edging.
- Photocopy or scan an old, patterned fabric or wall covering, patterns from dishes, or anything else that belonged to the person you are trying to bring alive in your scrapbook.

Resource

See what the editors of *Memory Makers* accomplished using actual quilt designs in *Quilted Scrapbooks* (Memory Makers, 2001).

KEEP IT SIMPLE

If you are overwhelmed by the variety of options and materials, take a deep breath and focus on a simple design using the following:

- Embossed paper (some even provide openings for photographs)
- Lettering
- Images as your focus
- Border cuts or paper cuts for decoration
- A blank space for viewers of your album to write their comments

These tips will also make your album look timeless, rather than dated, even in the future.

DIGITAL SCRAPBOOKS

So what do you need to create a heritage album—family history, photographs, memorabilia, and some scrapbook supplies. Right? Well that's a good start, but what about a scanner, digital camera, an internet connection and some software. You're probably thinking, "Huh?" The world of scrapbooking is not only a hands-on craft but one that is computer generated. Join one of the newest scrapbooking trends and create a digital rather than paper album by using web sites and software. There's even a new term for the technique: e-scrapbooking.

To create heritage pages and albums using your computer you'll need imagination, a few tools, a creative spirit and a willingness to try new things. You don't need to be a specialist in computer graphics or even a lot of images to create interesting heritage albums. Many of the heritage layouts use a single image as a focal point.

Your computer must have adequate storage capacity to handle graphics software and whatever peripheral devices you decide you need, like digital cameras and scanners. An Internet connection allows you to share your creations via e-mail or take your e-scrapbooking to the next level by posting a family Web site of your pages. When you think about it, what's a family home page, but a scrapbook online?

If you want to show off your work and get praise (and constructive criticism) from other scrappers then post your pages online at <www.twopeas inabucket.com> or <www.scrapbook ing.com> and see what others think. Look at their pages for inspiration and email those individuals for advice and construction tips.

Software

To create a digital heritage album you need to invest in image-editing software that allows you to improve the look of a heritage photo, enhance the look of an old document or even create pages on your computer. Basic image editing packages come with digital cameras and scanners, but might not include all the features you need. Carefully read the system requirements to make sure they are compatible with your computer.

Alpha Cupps. This layout was entirely created using Ulead Photo Impact 8, including the photo corners, eyelets, and paper. The army seal is clip art available at web-clipart.about.com. Credit: Sharon Collins.

Software like Adobe Photoshop 7.0 is intended for professional use. Its price places it out of reach of most average computer users and it has a steep learning curve. In order to become adept, you'll have to learn a new vocabulary and techniques. Go to any bookstore and see how many publications focus on teaching Photoshop. That's an indication of the amount of time you'll spend learning about the product. There are plenty of other choices including Microsoft's Picture It! that comes in several different versions such as Platinum or Digital Image Pro. Adobe's PhotoShop Elements and Ulead's Photo Impact programs offer an incredible amount of features and cost about the same as Microsoft's Digital Image Pro. They are affordable and most people find them easy to use. Read reviews like those on ConsumerSearch.com before you purchase any program. Many digital scrapbook enthusiasts start with one program and then graduate to another. Once you buy a program, play with it until you're comfortable with the features it offers.

One beauty of photo-editing software is that you can change history. You can remove sections of photographs (including annoying relatives) and paste them back together however you like. However, don't take these changes lightly especially in a heritage album. As a historian I like to represent history as it occurred without too much tinkering, but the tools are there if you need them.

Cameras

Digital cameras have several advantages. You can take the camera with you to a relative's house and make copies of family photographs, or you can visit the cemetery and have pictures of the headstones that you can download to your computer and use in your heritage pages that day. Going to a family reunion? Take the camera with you and e-mail copies of pictures to relatives without any extra cost. Select images for use in your scrapbook page from your photo editing software and you're on your way.

Purchasing criteria includes more than price. Make sure that the camera fits your needs. Try it out at the camera store and read reviews before purchasing one. Online reviews like those at Steve's Digicams <www. steves-digicams.com> can help you make the right decision. The key word in this technology is *megapixels* or *resolution*. The average resolution of images on the web is VGA (640 x 480 pixels), but if you intend to make traditional prints for your heritage albums you'll want to buy a camera with at least two megapixels (1600 x 1200 pixels) for crisp looking prints.

When purchasing a camera, ask what peripherals you'll need. Can you connect it directly to your computer or do you need a separate memory card reader? Does the memory card included with the camera have enough storage capacity for your needs or should you purchase a larger one? While most cameras use regular batteries, a set of rechargeable ones is a good investment. What may start out seeming like an inexpensive camera can become surprisingly costly when you add up all the extras. So, make sure you understand your camera needs and add up the final charges before you make that purchase.

Scanners
Add details to your pages by scanning designs from heirloom objects, old magazines or even elements from old photographs such as mats and backgrounds. You can use the textured paper of old photographic sleeves as the "paper" in your digital layouts or create "paper" using a photo editing program.

OTHER CREATIVE HELPS

Think about the elements that are part of a hands-on heritage page. The basic pieces—paper, fonts or journaling, photographs, tags—all come together in a layout.

Digital scrapbooking, the art of manipulating images and text to create a scrapbook page on your computer with simple tools and software can invigorate your albums. Whether you choose to use just digital manipulation or a combine it with hands-on layout, you'll be sure to find new ways to express yourself with some of these tips.

• Just getting started? Try ready made layouts like those from Wendi Speciale's company <www.anklebiter.com> or those in Scrapbook Factory Deluxe from Nova Development.

• Improve the quality of family photographs or restore faded or damaged images.

• Add clip art from books, CD-ROMs or find it free on the Internet.

• Scan an old, patterned fabric or wall covering, patterns from dishes or anything else that belonged to the person you are trying to bring alive in your scrapbook.

• Use e-papers to provide a background for your images and text rather than just color.

• Create your own background by scanning elements from photographs and handwritten documents. For instance, use an ancestor's handwriting to make your own digital paper or use designs from photographs to add new frames to your pictures.

• Miss the look of old albums with "scotch taped" corners? You can recreate the look with photo editing software.

• Fill blank space with journaling, clipart or memorabilia.

• Find free fonts and clip art online

• Take pictures of items too large to fit into your heritage album and use them as digital images.

• Make a completely digital page or just use some of the techniques to add color and details to your hand crafted scrapbook pages.

E-scrapbooking lets you take your genealogy to a new level of creativity. Make gifts, pages, albums or even websites to share with your family. All from your computer! The digital community is waiting for your additions.

Inspiration is only a mouse click away. View creations posted online and add your interpretation. You won't believe what you'll be able to accomplish! Whether you choose to entirely use digital manipulation or a combine it with hands-on layout, you'll be sure to find new ways to express yourself.

PRESERVING YOUR DIGITAL CREATIONS

Unfortunately, there are preservation issues with digital as well as hand-crafted albums. If you consistently backup your picture, data files and heritage album creations then congratulate yourself. You deserve it. If not, follow these few rules and repeat them like a mantra: I will back up my files; I will do it on a regular basis; I will make two copies of the backup. Two copies covers the just in case clause of computer operation. Store them in two separate places, protecting them from floods, heat, scratch-

es, and operator mistakes. If you click the wrong button you might inadvertently erase the disk or drive on which you store your pictures. Photo-CD's or zip drives work well as backup mediums. While CD's used to have a short shelf life (under 10 years) manufacturers now claim the disks last at least 50 years. Store your CD's in the same environment as your original photographs—at a temperature of no more than 77 degrees Fahrenheit and 40 percent humidity

Printing Concerns

If you chose to print out your computer creations there are several options: use a professional photo printing service; a home printer with special inks and papers; or one of the new printers that feature water-resistant, fade-resistant inks and special papers.

Should you decide to continue printing images at home, use products specifically manufactured for stability. Lyson Ltd. <www.lyson.com> and MIS Associates, Inc. <www.inksupply.com> can supply you with appropriate inks and papers. With consumer awareness of preservation issues increasing, more equipment manufacturers are advertising papers, inks and printing technologies to make prints that will last longer than ever before. Keep up with the latest research by looking at Henry Wilhelm's website, www.wilhelm research.com. You'll also find a list of suppliers. Wilhelm is co-author with Carol Brower of *The Permanence and Care of Color Photographs: Traditional and Digital Color Prints, Color Negatives, Slides and Motion Pictures* (Preservation Publishing Co, 1993). Storage considerations are the same as your disks and CDs—stable temperature and humidity. Remember to use albums constructed of acid and lignin-free paper as well as non-PVC plastic protectors. You'll want these digital creations to last for generations just like your hand-crafted albums.

SCHERENSCHNITTE

When considering various ways to tell your story, you might be surprised to discover that some of the items you're including have a history of their own. For instance, papercutting techniques like those used to highlight photographs or add interest actually date to 960 A.D in China. Called scherenschnitte, papercutting was a popular hobby in both Germany and Pennsylvania in the nineteenth century. Try re-creating some of these designs by following the directions offered at ←www.geocitieis.com/Heartland/Valley/8063/scherenschnitte.htm→ or purchase pre-made versions.

Gina Bear products duplicate the paper cuttings known as "scherenschnitte."

CHAPTER EIGHT

CREATING AN ALBUM FOR THE FUTURE

C reating scrapbooks is not a new hobby; our ancestors used their spare moments to lay out images and paper memorabilia in albums. Some of the more elaborate examples resemble contemporary scrapbooks in their use of clippings and related artwork. Unfortunately the techniques employed by our ancestors—and by many of today's scrapbook enthusiasts—are beautiful pictorial narratives of family history but a preservation nightmare.

Unless you use materials considered "archival," your heritage album may not last to be appreciated by future generations. Unknown to most people is that techniques recommended in some of the books on scrapbooking will keep photo and paper conservators busy for a long time. Sitting in archives and attics all over the country are scrapbooks in various stages of deterioration. There is a simple reason for this damage. All of the materials inherent to scrapbooks such as albums, papers, inks, and glues add up to a mess. For example, the glue used to paste the images into the albums has in most cases begun to seep through the pictures, or in other cases, made it impossible to remove the photographs from the pages. This doesn't need to be the case. By using a little common sense and a few basic rules, you can avoid the unknowing mistakes of past generations. By using products and avoiding certain behaviors, your albums can be appreciated by future generations. But how do you know if the techniques in the books and magazines are safe for your family photographs?

Archival: There is no industry standard for use of this term. It generally refers to materials that are acceptable for use in museums and libraries made from acid- and lignin-free materials.

There are major misconceptions in some scrapbooking manuals. Acid-free is not always archival. This terminology is overused. Archival refers to material that will not cause additional damage to your family heirlooms. It is important to read the labels and ask manufacturers for information about your supplies. When purchasing products, look for appropriate terms such as acid- and lignin-free, polypropylene, Mylar, or the following:

• *Creating Keepsakes* magazine uses an advisory committee of preservationists for products that receive their "CK OK" stamp of approval. A full list appears on the Web site <www.creating keepsakes.com/letsscrapbook/ck_ok>.

• "Archival" in the advertisement. Call the manufacturer for verification if it doesn't include details about its "archival qualities."

In response to the preservation standards advocated by leaders in the industry, many manufacturers now advertise and sell special products specifically for scrapbook enthusiasts. This means that anyone can create durable, safe, and attractive scrapbooks if they use the right materials. Keep up with new products by reading magazines that feature columns on safe products such as *Memory Makers* magazine and *Creating Keepsakes* magazine.

ALBUMS

In the late 1970s, I created a series of albums using the wrong materials. At the time I was unaware of the dangers of acidic paper and adhesives. Today those albums are in terrible shape. The acid and the glue in the magnetic album stained the images while the plastic overleaf disintegrated and stuck to the pictures. Today this type of damage is avoidable.

Anyone desiring to create a heritage album has a wide variety of choices. The best albums can be purchased from archival supply catalogs. While these cost more than the albums commonly available in discount stores, they are worth the investment. In general make sure the albums you decide to use have the following characteristics:

• The basic features of a preservation quality album are acid- and lignin-free paper and boards.

• Make sure that the adhesive and the covering that holds the album together are also acid-free. Authors Jeanne English and Al Thelin of *Saving Our Scrapbooks* (Creating Keepsakes, 1999) advise staying away from vinyl naugahyde because the resulting hydrogen chloride gas will destroy your images.

• Preservationists recommend selecting an album that comes with a slipcase to protect your images from light and dust.

• Make sure the album opens flat so that you don't put strain on your page layouts like one that's post-bound.

PAPER

Scrapbook paper and card stock comes in a variety of colors and textures. Most is labeled acid-free, but there are other things to verify that it is also archival. For instance, a piece of colored paper may be labeled acid-free, but archival papers will not bleed ink and dyes on your images. Another consideration is whether the paper is lignin-free. Naturally found in tree and plants, lignin is the substance that causes paper to yellow with age. While the acid added to paper during the production process to break down the wood chips causes staining, it is the lignin that helps to create the aged look that paper acquires when left in the sun.

WHAT ABOUT VELLUM?

Is vellum safe to use in your scrapbooks? While vellum used to refer to parchment (made from animal skin), the term now also is used to describe certain types of art papers. In general, vellum may contain chemicals that make them unsafe for use with photographs even if they are acid- and lignin-free. Consider using vellum in your album if it has the following qualities:

• Acid- and lignin-free
• Passes the Photographic Activity Test, meaning it was tested to see if it was photo-safe
• Color-fast
• Slightly buffered

Until the final word is out, keep vellum away from the front of your photographs and be careful using it with other items. It is still unknown how it reacts with materials other than photographs.

SKILL-BUILDING: TESTING PAPER QUALITY—PH AND BLEEDING COLORS

It is easy to check the acid content of paper. You can purchase a pH testing pen from the suppliers listed in the Appendix. If the line you draw on the paper with the testing pen turns purple, the paper is acid-free, which means it has a neutral pH (6.5-7.5) or the pH is higher than 7.0. The presence of other colors indicates that acid is present. It is necessary to use a pH testing strip and distilled water on darker paper.

Since the dyes in some paper bleed when exposed to water or high humidity, you need to test highly colored papers for stability. This is done by dropping a small dot of water on the paper or by placing a small piece of the paper in a cup of water. If the color comes off, then the paper is not approved for use in archival scrapbooks. For this reason some preservationists suggest using papers and cutouts of a neutral color. Fortunately these papers are available from library suppliers and most scrapbook stores.

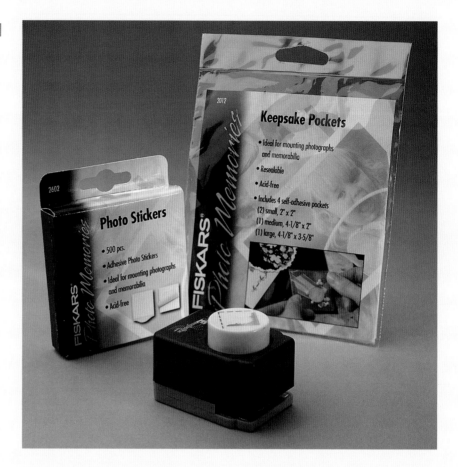

According to Gayle Humpherys in her article "Pulp Fact, Not Fiction" of *Creating Keepsakes* magazine (November 1999), there are four paper qualities that influence the preservation qualities of your scrapbook. Paper should be

- acid-free
- lignin-free
- buffered
- color-fast

ADHESIVES

Even if you use all acid-free albums, the techniques you employ to create the scrapbook may cause your project to fall apart or damage the images and documents. There are many books that suggest that scrapbooking actually preserves your images and then tell you to use glue, paint, and other harmful materials as part of your project. I've seen all types of damage caused by the use of adhesives and advocate that scrapbook hobbyists use photo corners for affixing images to pages rather than any type of glue, including those advertised as safe and archival.

OTHER OPTIONS

• Photo corners range from clear Mylar to decorative paper corners. Either is recommended for use in albums as long as the materials are archival. Remember that paper corners need to be acid- and lignin-free. Clear corners can be made of the two types of plastics approved for use with images: Mylar or polypropylene. When a manufacturer states its corners are made out of plastic, you need to verify that they are one or the other. If in doubt, ask the supplier. Place any type of memorabilia or paper documents in a polypropylene sleeve or encapsulate before including them in your album.

• All photo corners use an adhesive that doesn't come in contact with the images or documents, but you want to make sure that it is reversible, colorless, odorless, solid, and acid-free. Unless you are using copies of all your images and documents, it is best to refrain from placing cutouts and stickers on them, no matter how safe the manufacturer claims they are. A good rule is never use any technique that can't be undone. In other words, be careful with your originals. Once they are damaged, it could be costly or impossible to repair.

• Another option is to purchase a special paper punch that allows you to create slits in your pages to hold the photographs or documents by their corners. This eliminates the need for special supplies and concerns about adhesives. Unfortunately, if a document or image is fragile, the corners of the items can fall off from being placed on the album page.

SKILL-BUILDING: REMOVING OLD ADHESIVE

If you need to remove adhesive from the back of photographs or remove items from an old album, you can use Un-du Adhesive Remover by Doumar Products (888) 289-8638 ←www.un-du.com→. It has been rated safe by Rochester Institute of Technology, Duke University, and *Creating Keepsakes*. This non-abrasive substance removes most adhesives by neutralizing them. Place a few drops on the area and use a clean, soft, lint-free cloth to gently wipe away the adhesive, working from the middle to the edges. This will prevent you from bending the image during the process. Un-du is quick-drying.

SKILL-BUILDING: DISASSEMBLING MAGNETIC ALBUMS

Using a simple piece of dental floss, you can remove material from a magnetic photo album. This type of album has strips of adhesive on the page with a plastic sheet protector. Gently holding the floss the way you would to clean your teeth, slide it underneath the photograph or paper item. Move the floss slowly so as not to damage the item you are trying to remove.

INKS, PENS, AND MARKERS

Labeling your images is an important part of creating any type of heritage album. After all, you wouldn't want to spend the time to create the album and have a future generation be unable to identify the individuals because you didn't label the items. In general, all materials should be labeled by placing information underneath or alongside your pictures. (See Chapter 6 for additional captioning techniques.)

Remember that a basic caption includes the name of the person (with life dates), details about the event depicted, and some basic information on the material being added to your heritage scrapbook.

Here are a few guidelines for using inks in your heritage album.

• Never write on the front of the image or item. Use the page not the front of original items as labels.

• Never use a ballpoint pen or a felt-tip marker. The ballpoint smudges and makes indentations in the image, while a felt-tip marker's water soluble ink can be absorbed by the image. You can use a soft graphite pencil on the back while the image is face down on a hard clean surface, but never use anything on the picture area. Even if you are using copies, it is not a good idea to write on anything you add to your album. The pressure of the pencil will leave indentations in the surface of the item.

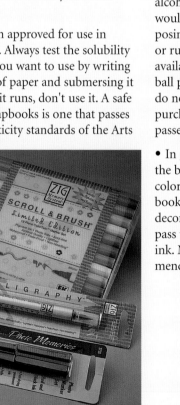

• Look for a pen with a soft tip and waterproof ink if you want to label the back of a resin-coated image like a contemporary photograph or the outside of a sleeved or encapsulated item. Just be sure to give the ink enough time to dry or you will end up with ink where you didn't intend it.

• Use a pen approved for use in scrapbooks. Always test the solubility of the ink you want to use by writing on a piece of paper and submersing it in water. If it runs, don't use it. A safe pen for scrapbooks is one that passes the non-toxicity standards of the Arts and Creative Materials Institute. They recommend that the ink be waterproof, fade resistant, permanent, odorless (when dry), and quick drying. Don't be concerned about the smell of the ink when wet, pens that dry rapidly often contain alcohol that dissipates when dry. You wouldn't want to spend hours composing an entry only to have it smudge or run. Most of the pens commonly available in stationery stores such as ball points, roller-balls, and markers do not meet these standards. Before purchasing a pen, try it out to see if it passes the test.

• In general, permanent black ink is the best choice for captioning since colored inks can fade. While scrapbook manuals advise using color for decorative features, make sure they pass the criteria for scrapbook-safe ink. Metallic inks are not recommended.

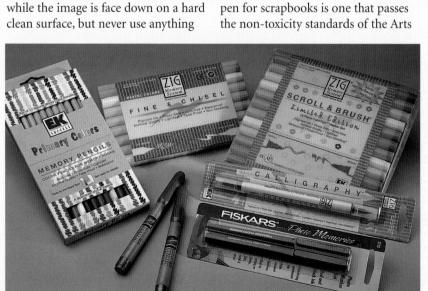

RUBBER STAMPING

Decorating pages with all types of graphic elements including rubber-stamped designs is part of what makes a scrapbook attractive. But is it safe? Preservation experts suggested that while most inks and materials are safe, no one knows if the image will fade and change color.

• Use inks that are safe for scrapbooks. Be sure to test the water solubility of the ink after it has dried.

• Use embossing powders that raise the stamped image as long as they don't come into contact with your original materials. In fact, embossing seals the ink and protects your heritage materials from the chemicals in the ink.

SHEET PROTECTORS

You have the option of protecting your scrapbook pages from mishandling by slipping them into sheet protectors. This also eliminates any abrasive damage that occurs when pages rub together. Just as it is important to consider the chemicals in paper, you should be aware of the best type of sheet protector. You wouldn't want to spend time and money buying scrapbook safe products only to undo your efforts with poor-quality plastics.

   Sheet protectors come in a variety of designs. Some are top loading, while others have pockets or fold-over edges. You can decide to forgo scrapbook papers in favor of using specially sized protectors. A list of suppliers is listed in the Appendix.

• Make sure that they are either Mylar/polyester or polypropylene. Both of these types of plastic do not deteriorate with time or deposit chemicals on your scrapbook pages. Don't use pages made from polyethylene

because of a chemical added during the manufacturing process. This "slip agent" helps the sheets move smoothly through production, but over time it rises to the surface of the pages where it can cause smudging.

• Since the weight of your scrapbook pages varies based on the paper you've selected, try different types of heavy-weight and medium-weight sheets to see which type suits your purposes. If your page is laden down with heavy photographs or objects, use heavy-weight sheet protectors to reinforce the page.

• Another issue is whether to use non-glare or clear pages. Again there is a preservation concern. Non-glare pages sometimes contain substances to give pages that appearance.

STICKERS

Stickers are fun and add to the visual interest of the scrapbook you are creating. Use them freely in your album, but make sure that they are acid- and lignin-free, including the adhesive. They can be used safely as long as you don't place them directly on documents and images.

NEVER LAMINATE ANYTHING

There is a common myth that won't die. Many people wrongly believe that laminating their documents will help preserve them. Initially lamination was thought to protect items. Unfortunately, once something is encased in laminate, damage begins to occur almost at once. The acid sealed inside and the plastic covering starts to deteriorate documents and photographs. Indeed, the entire process is harmful and irreversible. In addition, exposing items to heat during the lamination process ages the material. See pages 62-63 for the safe technique of encapsulation.

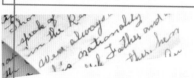

WAYS TO SAVE MONEY

If you don't watch out, putting together a heritage album can be an expensive undertaking. There are a few simple ways to save money and still create a beautiful keepsake.

Plan

Like all shopping ventures, you'll spend more if you don't make a list before you shop. Make sure you know what supplies you already have on hand. Do your research on products before leaving home by consulting magazines and vendor Web sites.

Look for Discounts

A specialty store may sell paper at one price and a large chain store might offer it for less. Try to find a bargain whenever you shop through price comparisons. Craft stores often have sales on specific items. You might find a special offer at a scrapbook convention.

Buy in Bulk

Large packages of paper or boxes of pens are often less expensive than purchasing them one at a time. Bring a calculator and do the math. Once you know what you need to complete the project, you'll be less likely to impulse purchase.

Keep Your Pages Simple

Your pages will be beautiful whether you use expensive extras or focus on the basics: photographs and information. Thinking through your project can help you save. Use the money you save to purchase a few extras to highlight your pages sparingly.

Share with Friends

Ask friends who scrapbook about the equipment they own, organize a crop night at your house, and share materials as a group. You'll all save and have a good time working together.

Remember that your heritage album is a reflection of your creativity and the family history you've collected. Only your imagination limits you!

FAMILY MEMORABILIA

Part of the process of creating a scrapbook is including the memorabilia that adds meaning to the events and people you are documenting. Unfortunately, the types of items you place in the album can adversely affect all the archival steps you've taken to protect your photographs. Documents transfer acid to the images, ink in fabric and yarns can bleed if it isn't colorfast, and flowers will stain. Leather is treated with tannic acid, which will leech onto your images, documents, and pages. So what materials can be included and how?

Documents and newspaper clippings add another dimension to the story you are trying to tell. However, since the paper is acidic, you want to be careful they don't come into contact with your images. Preservationists recommend de-acidification before placing them in scrapbooks. Seek the advice of an expert before attempting to use any of the de-acidification sprays on the market or immersing the documents in a special solution, in case parts of the document will be damaged by the solution. Another option is to make copies on acid- and lignin-free papers.

We all have small pieces of material we would like to include in the story of our lives from naturally based items like flowers, rocks, and ceramics to plastic objects such as the little trinkets you pick up while you are on vacation or that your children bring home. Unfortunately, natural objects transfer lignin and acid to your scrapbook pages, plastics give off gases, and rock and ceramics are abrasive. Money is also unsuitable for inclusion until it is cleaned and placed in a protective covering. However, there is hope.

• Encapsulation is safe and reversible—exactly the opposite of

lamination. Before encapsulating any document, make sure that it has been de-acidified using special solutions. This can be used for items too large for ready-made envelopes and sleeves. See instructions in Chapter 3.

• Include memorabilia by using specially made polypropylene envelopes that use the same adhesive as the corners. They are available in a variety of sizes from scrapbook suppliers. Some scrapbook suppliers have products that offer creative solutions such as storage compartments and decorative frames. Be sure to check with the manufacturer to ensure that the plastics these items are made from are either polypropylene or Mylar.

There are materials that you can safely include in your album such as most fabrics and yarns as long as they are acid-free, non-abrasive, and color-fast. When in doubt about whether an object or item is safe, include it in a protective covering to be sure you are not inadvertently causing damage.

There are so many new products on the market that it is difficult to keep current with the latest preservation concerns.

Basic rules for safe scrapbooking include not placing anything in direct contact with an original image or document just in case the item eventually causes damage. Children's drawings can be included as long as you place them in appropriate plastic sleeves first. Make sure the rest of the items aren't abrasive and are color-fast. If you are unsure about any item, either don't use it, find a substitute (like using photo safe ink instead of embroidery floss), or consult the "CK OK" list at www.creatingkeepsakes.com/letsscrapbook/ck_ok/.

BASIC RULES OF SCRAPBOOKING

Golden Rule: Don't cause any permanent damage to your irreplaceable heritage materials

Do's

1. Use scrapbook-safe materials.
2. Use copy photos, placing originals in storage.
3. Enhance the value of your album by labeling the images.
4. Use materials that are of good quality.
5. Do create a lasting artifact that future generations can enjoy.

Don'ts

1. Don't use magnetic albums with adhesive pages.
2. Never crop original photographs or cut documents.
3. Never write on the front of any original item.
4. Don't include materials that are of poor quality or in disrepair.
5. Don't place adhesive directly on an item or attach cutouts.

CONSULT THE EXPERTS

If you need advice, look no further than two popular magazines, *Creating Keepsakes* and *Memory Makers*. If you don't know where to buy supplies or attend classes in your area, consult the directories in the back of every issue. To keep track of current trends and new products, consider becoming a member of the International Scrapbook Trade Association. Members receive a bimonthly newsletter.

TOOLKIT FOR A SAFE SCRAPBOOK

• Album with acid-free pages. These can be ordered from several of the suppliers mentioned in the Appendix, purchased through a local scrapbook store or from an online supplier.

• Polypropylene corners: Made of clear polypropylene with an adhesive back, they hold the photographs in place without putting the image in contact with the adhesive.

• Inks that are color-fast.

• Pens and markers that are water-proof, fade resistant, permanent, odor-less (when dry), and quick drying.

• Acid- and lignin-free papers and adhesives.

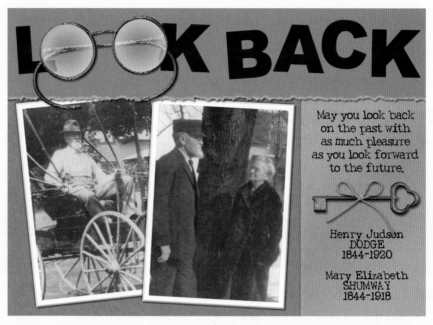

The paper and vellum were created in Paint Shop Pro. The quote is a Chinese proverb. The key and glasses are copyright 2003 by Kim Liddiard. Credit: Jenna Robertson.

MOEGLIN

3 June 1885 – Susan born in Little Falls, Minn.

17 December 1887 – Tillie born in Little Falls

16 September 1908 – Tillie marries William J. Billstein in Little Falls

1 June 1909 – Susan marries Henry Wyrwicki (later Smith) in Little Falls

6 August 1912 – Tillie and Henry move to Jamestown, ND.

1 January 1937 – Tillie dies of pneumonia in Jamestown

24 June 1961 – Susan dies of age in Little Falls

Susan Marie Moeglin
Mathilda "Tillie" Ann Moeglin

above: Susan (r) and Tillie, early 1889
right: Susan (r) and Tillie, 1903 or 1904

Paper—Anna Griffin; embossed oval frames—Canson; stickers, floral frame and flower cutouts—K+GO. Credit: Diane Haddad and Lynne Betlock.

CHAPTER NINE

ORGANIZING WHAT YOU DON'T USE

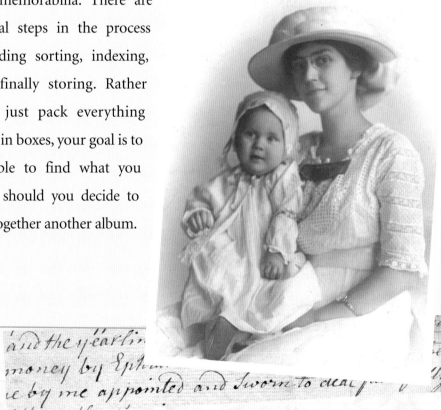

N ow that you've selected all the items you want to include in your heritage album, you're probably wondering what to do with all the excess material you've collected. Since only a small percentage of what you've located appears in the album, the next step is organizing the rest. It would be wonderful to be able to fit everything you find into one album, but unfortunately this isn't possible unless you have a very small collection of photographs, documents, artifacts, and memorabilia. There are several steps in the process including sorting, indexing, and finally storing. Rather than just pack everything away in boxes, your goal is to be able to find what you need should you decide to put together another album.

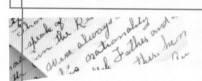

EASY REFERENCE STEPS

- Evaluate your collection.
- Develop an organizational system.
- Create a work space.
- Sort your collection according to system.
- Order supplies.
- Label, box, and index collection.
- Prepare suitable storage space for collection.

BASIC SUPPLIES

- Storage materials
- White cotton gloves for handling material
- Soft lead pencil
- Permanent markers for labeling objects

Organizing the rest of the materials you've gathered requires the same steps as putting together an album page. Here are the steps you followed to put together an album page. Compare them to the time savers on page 117.

- Finding the time
- Having a work space
- Sorting material
- Planning your organizational system
- Purchasing supplies
- Finishing the project

FINDING THE TIME

Keeping your organizational scheme simple and flexible requires a little pre-planning. One of the greatest time-wasters is reorganizing once you have started. This can use up hours of good work time.

Often the hardest part of organizing your family collection is finding the time to do it. However, by breaking the entire process down into a series of steps, it can be easily accomplished.

Use the same time-saving techniques you employed when putting together your heritage album. As you know, setting aside a half-hour here and there adds up until you are finished. Employ a basic rule of organization: Keep your system simple and flexible so that everyone who needs to use it can understand it. That's why it is important to streamline the process so that you avoid overwhelming yourself and users of the collection with complicated arrangements. Flexibility is a key element so that you can add new materials without having to reorganize.

Part of the planning process is evaluating your collection. Take into consideration the size, shape, and number of items you are organizing. Ask questions that help you assess the collection. First, think about how you use the materials. Do they sit in a closet untouched for months at a time or do you regularly go through them reminiscing about people and activities? If you are like most people you use some of the collection all of the time and only look at the rest occasionally. Each question helps identify storage needs and suggests ways to organize your collection. Don't become discouraged. This part of the process only takes a little while and will actually save you time later on.

SORTING AND ORGANIZING

There are a number of options for sorting and organizing from simply using surnames to entering everything into a computer program. There is one simple rule: Think through what you want to do so that you end up touching items only once. It's a good idea to lay out your plans on paper first, just like you did when you decided on the look of the heritage album. A little pre-planning will prevent you from making costly mistakes of time and money. Look at your organizational scheme as if you knew nothing about the individuals and items. Can you still find people and specific events? If you have trouble separating yourself from the information, ask a friend to look over your plan. See if they can understand how the materials relate to one another. If you are a hands-on person, try to organize a small part of your collection and see if it works. Pre-planning will provide you with a sense of size of the project you are undertaking.

CREATE A WORK SPACE

Whenever you are working with your family material, it is important to find a spot in the house where you can spread out and leave it undisturbed until the organizational project is complete. Remember that your work area needs to be clean and big enough to provide space for boxes and your other supplies. You can save time by having this area ready to use whenever you have a few moments. If you have to set up the area each work session, you will waste precious minutes to make progress. If space is at a premium, a card table in a corner of a room can be helpful. You can cover it with a clean cloth between sessions. Efficiency experts suggest having everything you need within reach to eliminate a major time-waster: looking for missing items.

SORTING

When you have an idea of the system you want to use and have tried it out with a few items, you are ready to start implementing your plan. Begin by sorting your material by type (photographs, manuscripts, artifacts) and surname. Since this is a family history project, it makes sense to organize material by surname rather than chronologically. Start by grouping materials by name (surname and first name) and placing them in boxes. Create a list of who is included so you know how many separate boxes you need for this part of the process. Bear in mind that there is no perfect solution. Each organizational method has problems that need to be overcome.

SUPPLIES

Looking through your collection helps you estimate storage needs. Follow the storage guidelines in the appropriate chapter for each type of material. Order materials from the archival suppliers listed in the Appendix. It is advisable to buy in bulk whenever possible since most suppliers offer discounts for quantity buying. Try asking a friend or a local historical society to share an order so that both of you save. Not sure how many boxes you need? Call the supplier or look at the description listed in his catalogs. Most will provide information on how many items fit comfortably in a box or album. All of the suppliers listed in the Appendix provide catalogs free of charge.

LABELING AND BOXING

Another time saver advised by efficiency experts is to only move a single piece of paper once. It is difficult to do with a variety of family memorabilia and artifacts, but if you apply their advice to labeling you'll be surprised how much progress you can make. Since there are many different ways to organize a collection keep it simple by arranging them alphabetically by name. If you used a genealogical software program or numbering system, you can use it to keep track of what you own by including photographs in the program. If you have a large and complex collection you may end up using more than one system depending on the types of materials in your possession.

TIME SAVERS

1. Have an organizational plan.
2. Stay focused.
3. Prepare a work area.
4. Keep everything handy.
5. Work on one task at a time.

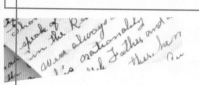

STORING YOUR COLLECTION

Keep in mind that you need to find a proper storage place for your collection. An ideal spot is a windowless closet away from heat sources and water pipes.

TYPES OF FILING SYSTEMS

There are several different types of indexes, from card files to inventories and computer programs. Each has strengths and weaknesses, but all have the same purpose. They help you find the item you need when you need them. While creating an index takes time, you will save minutes if not hours when you begin looking for something.

• *Color coding:* A simple way to organize material is by using different colors to signify various surnames or types of material.

• *Surname:* Create separate files for each surname with subheadings for each person or couple broken down by photographs, documents, and memorabilia (in this file would reside pictures of the items).

Heritage Album Tip:

Number the pages of your scrapbook and include the name of your album and the pertinent page number for material on family members in your index.

• *Card index:* There are plenty of people who rely on index cards to keep track of things. Create a card for each family member and list what you own and the box number it is kept in. Remember to include the full name of the person and life dates. Put maiden names in parentheses. This is a simple system that uses index or other size cards with information. It resembles a library card catalog in telling you what can be found where. Each card has a single name, life dates as well as where certain items can be found. These cards can immediately direct you to the appropriate box rather than having to look through three boxes. You can even color code the family cards if you want. Just to avoid any confusion, make a card for each woman you have material for under both her married name(s) and maiden name. Make a cross reference on one card to the other.

The weakness with any card file system is that the cards tend to get misfiled and can become jumbled if they are dropped. You can remedy the latter problem by using a large ring or an old card catalog drawer that has a rod running down the center of the drawer to hold the cards in place.

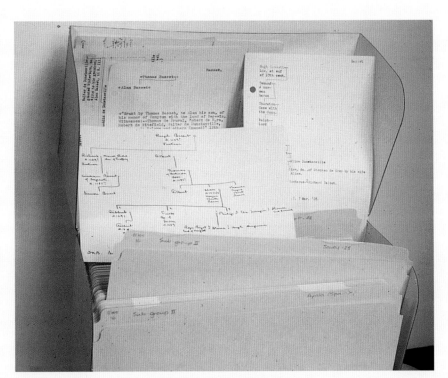

Utilize some of the same techniques that museums and archives use.
New England Historic Genealogical Society.

THE BASICS

Boxes
- Acid-free with reinforced corners or baked enamel cabinets

Paper
- Acid- and lignin-free

Plastic
- Polypropylene or Mylar

Inventories

Most museums and archives use inventories to keep track of one related collection. It is merely a guide to all the different types of material in the collection. If you have twelve different boxes and all of them contain different types of items owned by family members, think about how you are going to locate what you need quickly. An inventory enables you to do that.

There are several key parts to an inventory such as organizational scheme, provenance, and index. The first part of the inventory explains your system so that others understand it. Suppose a family member can only find eight of the twelve boxes. Your explanation tells them that they are missing four more. If you have managed to keep it simple, it will be easy to explain. The provenance of a collec-tion describes how the materials came to be in your collection. One of the most fascinating parts of a photograph collection is how it is passed on within a family. There appear to be no rules of inheritance when it comes to images, so it is important for others to understand how all the pieces fit. You need to explain how different parts of the collection came together. The final part is the index. In this you mention the name of each person and in which box, folder, or album the images are located.

The key ingredient to any arrange-ment is flexibility. You are using the same principles that professional archivists and librarians implement with collections in their facilities. Instead of assigning record group numbers, you are using surnames.

SOFTWARE

There are many different types of software on the market that can help you organize your collection of family material. Since your project is of a family history nature, why not use the products already at your disposal. By using a genealogical software package, you are connecting your images, documents, and information within a single program.

Genealogical Software Packages

There are special considerations to bear in mind when purchasing or using various packages or Web-based products. The key features you should look for in a program are price, computer requirements, ease of use, source documentation, file management, reports, and research help. If you are using the program to help you manage your photo files, you should purchase a program that also has the multimedia features you need. Evaluate each program before you purchase it to determine if it suits your needs. Consult the list in Chapter 10.

General Software Programs

There are many ways to organize your images using a computer. You can use everything from a word-processing program to create an index to your filing system of originals (very helpful with group portraits) to a database to "catalog" your items using information and pictures. There are several special programs on the market for organizing images, but before purchasing anything, find out if they do what you want by reading reviews. Ultimately it all depends on how sophisticated you want to get, your level of expertise, and what you want to spend on a program.

Resources

Need help organizing all that family history paperwork? Consult Sharon DeBartolo Carmack's *Organizing Your Family History Search: Efficient & Effective Ways to Gather and Protect Your Genealogical Research* (Betterway Books, 1999).

STORAGE CONSIDERATIONS

Of primary importance is where you store your collection. Can you think of any place in your house that is a constant temperature, has low humidity, is dark, and is out of the way of the hazards mentioned below? In most homes, the best place to store collections is on a shelf in a windowless closet that is not on an exterior wall (subject to temperature fluctuations). The worst places to store images are basements and attics. Try to find an appropriate spot in your house.

Avoid These Storage Areas

1. Basements: In many areas of the United States there is too much humidity and the possibility of a flood. A woman placed all her boxes of photographs in the basement when they were renovating their house. Unfortunately for her, when a major rainstorm hit the area, her basement flooded. Instead of calling a conservator for advice, she lost all of those pictures.

2. Attics: They experience extreme temperature fluctuations: Cold in the winter and hot in the summer.

3. Garages: They expose your photographs to humidity, temperature fluctuations, and toxic fumes.

Containers

There are many suppliers for special boxes, sleeves, and envelopes, but how do you know which ones are best for your images? You want to select materials that are guaranteed to protect your images. Some types of family heirlooms such as clothing require special handling and storage. In general paper and photographic items require materials that are acid- and lignin-free.

Plastics cause a whole array of problems for storage, so make sure that you buy ones made out of polypropylene or Mylar. Either is fine, but Mylar is more expensive. Polyethylene is not approved for long-term storage. Not all suppliers carry polypropylene or Mylar sleeves, so verify the materials beforehand by calling the supplier directly. Suppliers that are accustomed to working with libraries and museums will readily address your concerns.

Since plastic, wood, and regular acidic cardboard give off gases that cause a variety of problems, don't use containers made out of these substances to store your family treasures. The best materials are acid-free boxes with reinforced corners which are available from archival suppliers. Museums and libraries also use baked enamel metal cabinets for storage. Make sure the box tops fit snugly so that dirt and dust do not settle on your prints.

What to Avoid

1. Plastic or cardboard boxes. If the storage container gives off an odor there are gases being given off that will damage the images over time. Additionally the glue in the cardboard may seep onto the images and stain them.

2. Acid paper folders or envelopes. This includes brown craft paper and glass-

ine. There are several dangers. The chemicals used to bleach papers may cause the photographs to fade. If you place photographs in gummed envelopes, the glue can cause stains. The acid papers will, over time, stain the images as well.

3. Do not use rubber bands, paper clips, or other objects to keep your images together. Rubber bands deteriorate and adhere to the surface of the photograph while paper clips rust and cause indentations in the images.

4. Never laminate anything. Lamination increases the rate of deterioration.

How to Select Storage Materials
• Deal with a reputable supplier. See the list in the Appendix.

• For most items use acid- and lignin-free paper or boxes.

• If buying plastic sleeves, make sure they are polypropylene or Mylar.

CHAPTER TEN

TAKING YOUR RESEARCH BEYOND THE ALBUM

The heritage album you've compiled might encourage you to pursue genealogy as another hobby. If so you'll need a little more background in how it's done, when to ask for help, and how to find it. Who knows? You might decide to turn your discoveries into a book or an article. Family history is full of choices and fascinating facts.

Chapter 1 introduced you to family history, but the focus was on basic information, documents, photographs, and memorabilia that could be easily incorporated into a heritage album. This chapter helps you delve deeper into your family using other sources to trace your family history: city directories, probate, military, and court records, and immigration documents. Learn how genealogists use numbering systems and computer programs to keep track of their research. If you find yourself hooked on genealogy, you're not alone. It is considered one of the most popular hobbies in the United States.

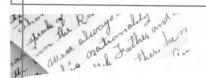

GENEALOGY PUBLICATIONS

By reading a wide variety of genealogical magazines, newsletters, and online e-zines, it's easy to keep up with the latest family history news or learn new techniques to help you solve your research problems. Consult ←www.cyndislist.com→ for a more extensive list and links.

American Genealogist

← www.americangenealogist.com→ Published since 1972, this scholarly magazine offers articles that analyze family history research problems.

Ancestry and Genealogical Computing

←www.ancestry.com→ Two print magazines published by MyFamily.com. Ancestry.com offers a free newsletter, "The Daily News," featuring columns by leading genealogists.

Eastman's Online Genealogy Newsletter

←www.rootsforum.com→ One of the oldest online e-zines, Dick Eastman's weekly newsletter keeps readers up-to-date on important topics for genealogists.

Family Tree Finders

←www.sodamail.com→ An e-zine written by genealogist and author, Rhonda McClure, on family history topics.

Family History News

←www.galethompson.freeserve.co. uk/familyhistorynews.htm→ Learn about new books and Web sites for research in the United Kingdom and beyond.

Family Tree Magazine

←www.familytreemagazine.com→ Print magazine published six times a year; free weekly newsletter available on the Web site.

Heritage Quest

←www.heritagequest.com→ Print magazine published bi-monthly; also offers a free weekly newsletter and message boards online.

National Genealogical Society Quarterly

Scholarly magazine offered by the National Genealogical Society ←www.ngsgenealogy.org→. Subscribe to the free news e-zine via the Web site.

New England Historical and Genealogical Register

←www.newenglandancestors.org→ Published quarterly by the New England Historic Genealogical Society and free to members along with a subscription to bi-monthly print newsmagazine, *New England Ancestors*. Subscribe to the free e-zine via the Web site.

NEW ENGLAND HISTORIC GENEALOGICAL SOCIETY

MAGAZINES, NEWSLETTERS AND E-ZINES

Finding out how to use specialized resources might mean reading magazines or meeting other family historians. Both are easy to do. There are several magazines or free e-newsletters that help keep you up to date. As for meeting other family historians, you can attend a lecture at a local genealogical society or attend a national conference.

There are additional resources to assist you in your family history search including city directories, probate records, and court documents. If you want to discover more unusual research sources, consult *Hidden Sources* by Laura Szucs Pfeiffer (Ancestry, 2000).

CITY DIRECTORIES

There are at least three types of directories that help you trace your ancestors in addition to telephone directories (phone books) and professional directories (membership lists):

• *City directories:* listing of individuals (by surname) and businesses in a community.

• *House directories:* listing of individuals and businesses by street address.

• *Business directories:* listing of businesses in a community or region.

Unless your family came from an urban area you won't be able to find them in all three types of directories. Business directories can also be found after the individual listing in a city directory. The first city directory in the United States was published in Philadelphia in 1785. You can find city directories in public libraries, historical societies, and even online at <www.ancestry.com>. If you want to learn more about using directories for family history search, consult Gordon Lewis Remington's chapter "Research in Directories" in Loretto Dennis Szucs' *The Source: A Guidebook of American Genealogy* (Ancestry, 1997).

SKILL-BUILDING: DIRECTORIES

Trace your family in the city directories looking for each member of the household.

Discover:
• Their occupation
• Who they worked for
• Deaths
• Track their moves on a local map using color stickers (include this in your album)

Directory research provides you with a year-by-year accounting of your ancestors' whereabouts and provides clues to locate land records, vital records, and employment details.

COMMON ABBREVIATIONS IN DIRECTORIES

• r or house: residence can refer to home ownership.
• bds: boards; or rents a room from owner of house.
• remd: removed; usually lists where the family moved to.

PROBATE RECORDS

When people die, they leave a lot of information in their wills. You can find evidence of adoptions and guardianships, as well as personal and real estate property. Family relationships become clearer when the deceased mentions their relationship to particular individuals. Probate records can be found on the city and town level in New England and on the county level in the rest of the country. The records are generally found where the death occurred if that was the primary residence.

IMMIGRATION DOCUMENTS

Every family with immigrant ancestors has a story based on the immigration experience. Many families insist that their ancestor's name was changed at Ellis Island or another port of arrival. That myth needs to be put to rest. While it's true that the surname your ancestor used in the old country may not be the same as the one you have today, there are plenty of reasons why that happened. The most common was that immigrants changed their names to make it easier to spell or understand during the assimilation process. Many foreign language names became an Anglicized equivalent. If you are looking for evidence linking your ancestor to their original homeland and didn't find any evidence in the other material you collected, try the following:

Passenger arrival lists: A list of the individuals on a particular ship and day; includes a record of border crossings.

Naturalizations: Immigrants intending to become citizens filed petition papers after a certain residency, and if approved, received citizenship papers. At certain points in American history, American-born citizens lost their citizenship when they married a non-citizen. In order to apply for citizenship, individuals listed their date of arrival, the ship they traveled on, the date and place of birth, and the names of a couple of witnesses.

Resources

• *A Genealogist's Guide to Discovering Your Immigrant and Ethnic Ancestors* by Sharon DeBartolo Carmack (Betterway Books, 2000)

• *They Became Americans: Finding Naturalization Records and Ethnic Origins* by Loretto Dennis Szucs (Ancestry, 1998)

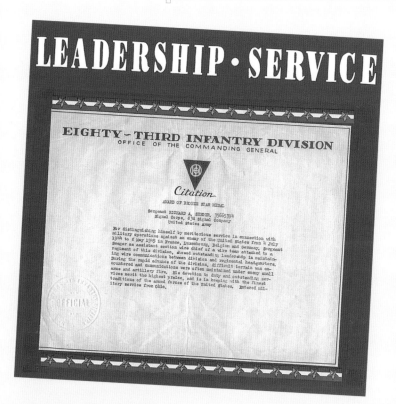

MILITARY DOCUMENTS

According to James C. Neagles, author of *United States Military Records*, in order "to locate military records for any individual, it is essential to know when and where in the armed forces he or she served and whether that person served in the enlisted ranks or was an officer." His advice applies whether your ancestor fought in a colonial conflict, in United States armed forces, or in a foreign country. First, determine who in your family tree was likely to have served. Then discover what military event they could have participated in. Once you've identified likely suspects and where they were living, you have a chance of finding their military records. Some will be located on the national level, others in local archives, and sometimes both. Colonial records are usually found in state and local archives and libraries. Military service questions appeared on several federal population censuses in particular:

• *1840:* asked the names of pensioners.

• *1850 to the present:* include occupations.

• *1890:* included a special census for Union Veterans and widows. Unfortunately, the majority of returns were destroyed in a fire.

• *1910:* asked individuals if they were Union or Confederate veterans.

• *1920:* military bases were supposed to be enumerated separately, but it did not happen in every case.

Resources

• *U. S. Military Records: A Guide to Federal & State Sources* by James C. Neagles (Ancestry, 1994)

• *How to Locate Anyone Who Is or Has Been in the Military* by Lt. Col. Richard S. Johnson and Debra Johnson Knox (MIE Publishing, 1999)

MORE RESOURCES

Many of the records mentioned in this chapter are on microfilm and can be borrowed from a Family History Library (FHL) in your area or used at the Family History Library in Salt Lake City, Utah. Consult the ←www.familysearch.org→ to find a FHL near you. A guide to the resources of the Family History is Paula Stuart Warren and James W. Warren's *Your Guide to the Family History Library* (Betterway Books, 2001).

COURT RECORDS

Was your ancestor a scoundrel? Civil and criminal court documents reveal family information in divorce records, criminal proceedings, and simple arguments over property. Depositions provide evidence of the problem and often clarify family relationships.

NUMBERING SYSTEMS

What's in a number? More than you might realize. If there is one thing that generates more questions, it is how to keep track of all those ancestors. Well, there are many different types of numbering systems used by professional genealogists. If you are having trouble finding an agreeable system, purchase a software program and let it number your ancestors. There are a variety of numbering systems used by family historians. Richard A. Pence discusses them in his article "Numbering Systems in Genealogy" <www.saint clair.org/numbers>. Here are two options:

Register System
Based on descendants in which the immigrant ancestor is number 1. Only individuals having children are numbered in subsequent generations.

Ahnentafel Numbering
("Ahnentafel" means ancestor in German.) Each person has a unique number based on his place in the pedigree chart. You are number 1, your parents are numbers 2 and 3. Basically, double an ancestor's number to get his father and add 1 to find his mother.

GENEALOGICAL SOFTWARE

If you're the type of person who likes to use a pencil and paper, then either skip this section or be enticed to use a software package. Computer programs keep track of those pesky genealogical numbering systems and can even connect you to online data resources. One of the nice things about using genealogy software, besides helping you stay organized, is that most programs offer a variety of charts. You just pick the one you like and print it out. You decide what information to include right down to the number of generations. There are plenty of options for every budget (including some free ones) and even for the technology-wary. Before purchasing any software, evaluate its features including its compatibility with your computer or other family history software you're using. Don't forget to read reviews and talk to friends.

• *Ancestral Quest 2002*
(Incline Software)
(800) 825-8864
<www.ancquest.com>
Download the latest version or purchase it as a package.

• *Ancestry Family Tree*
(MyFamily.com)
(800) 262-3787
<aft.ancestry.com>
Download free. If you're a member of Ancestry.com, the software matches names in your files with possible ancestors in its databases.

• *Family Origins*
(Formal Soft)
(866) 436-3526
<www.formalsoft.com>
Has one of the best Web-publishing options.

• *Family Tree Legends*
(Pearl Street Software)
<www.familytreelegends.com>
Backs up your files to a secure server, updates your online family tree, and scans the net.

• *Family Tree Maker 10*
(Genealogy.com)
(800) 548-1806
<www.familytreemaker.com>
One of the oldest genealogical software packages on the market includes outstanding charting capabilities.

• *Legacy Family Tree 4.0*
(Millennia Corp.)
(800) 753-3453
<www.legacyfamilytree.com>
Purchase on CD-ROM or download from the Web site.

• *The Master Genealogist*
(Wholly Genes)
(877) 864-3264
<www.whollygenes.com>
Many professional genealogists use this program because of its sophisticated features.

• *Personal Ancestral File 5.2*
(Salt Lake Distribution Center)
(800) 537-5950
<www.familysearch.org>

Download for free or purchase for a nominal fee on CD-ROM.

Software for MAC users

• *GEDitCOM 3.11*
(RSAC Software)
<www.geditcom.com>
Requires Mac OS 8.1 or higher.

• *Personal Ancestral File 5.2*
(see above)

• *Reunion 8.0*
(Leister Productions)
(717) 697-1378
<www.leisterpro.com>
Only software with a variety of features for Mac users.

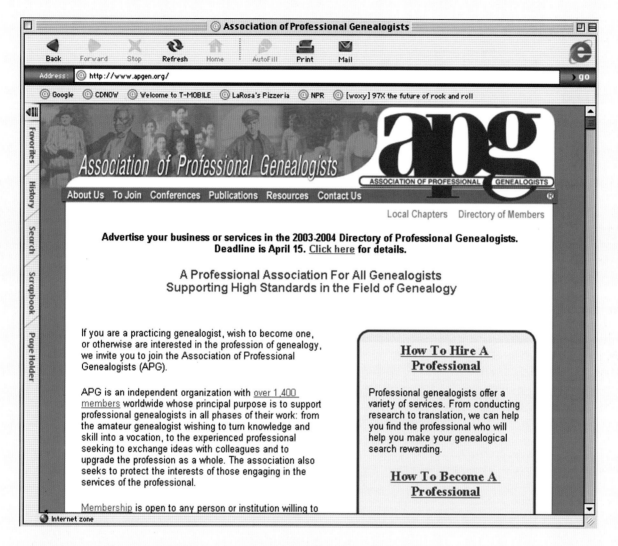

JOINING A LINEAGE SOCIETY

If you want to join a lineage society whose members trace their ancestry back to a specific group like the Daughters of the American Revolution, investigate its guidelines and requirements for membership. Most require proof of your lineage in the way of copies of original documents. Some organizations have volunteers or staff that can answer general application questions. A list of lineage societies appears in <www.cyndislist.com> under "Societies and Groups—Lineage."

ASKING FOR HELP

No matter how hard you try, you may find yourself unable to solve a research problem and need expert assistance. Many state and local historical societies keep lists of researchers that are available for hire. You can also look at a national directory of the Association of Professional Genealogists online at <www.apgen.org>. Even professionals hire assistance when looking for individuals in an area they are unfamiliar with.

WRITING YOUR FAMILY HISTORY

Think about taking all the information you've compiled and publishing it in a family history. It's just another way to present your family story in words and pictures. Some resemble formal genealogies incorporating numbering systems and including a few images, while others are written in a narrative format. You can decide to write a whole book or just focus on one interesting problem. Publish it yourself or have a press print it for you. Today there are more choices than ever for publishing your book from electronic publishing to traditional hardcover books. If you've never written a genealogy before, working with a specialized publisher will mean that your research will be formatted correctly and that you'll receive guidance throughout the process. After all, you'll want to be proud of your efforts and present it to interested family.

• **Gateway**
<www.gatewaypress.com>
This is one of the oldest genealogy vanity presses. They offer online guidance and advice for first time authors.

• **Newbury Street Press**
<www.newenglandancestors.com>
Newbury Street Press is part of the New England Historic Genealogical Society. The staff works with an editorial team of writers, designers, and genealogists to produce a family history for clients.

Resources

• *Genealogical Writing in the 21st Century: A Guide to Register Style and More* edited by Henry Hoff (NEHGS, 2002)

• *Producing a Quality Family History* by Patricia Law Hatcher (Ancestry, 1996)

• *You Can Write Your Family History* by Sharon DeBartolo Carmack (Betterway Books, 2003)

As you've learned how to locate everything you need for a heritage album, you've also acquired a new hobby—genealogy or family history. I'll bet that uncovering new information on your family has encouraged you to discover more. The nice thing about family history is that it is a lifelong pursuit that you can pass on to future generations. Whether you decide to create a series of heritage pages or work with relatives to produce a written family history, remember to enjoy your personal detective search for those elusive ancestors. I know I do!

SUPPLIERS

Most of the phone numbers are for wholesale purchasing. Check Web sites for retailers in your area or order direct online.

Anna Griffin, Inc.
(888) 817-8170
<www.annagriffin.com>
Offers beautiful papers and albums with a heritage theme.

CKC Creations
(888) 451-8080

C-Line Products, Inc.
Mt. Prospect, IL
(888) 860-9120
Sheet protectors.

Colorbok
<www.colorbok.com>
Stickers, albums, and more for heritage albums.

C-Thru Ruler Company
(800) 243-8419
<www.cthruruler.com>

EK Success
(800) 524-1349
<www.eksuccess.com>
The online catalog covers everything from stickers to special pens.

Family Treasures
24922 Anza Dr., Unit A
Valencia, CA 91355
(800) 413-2645
<www.commercemarketplace.com/home.scrapbooking>
Provides a full line of scrapbook supplies including paper punches, corners, papers, and pens.

Fiskars
7811 W. Stewart Ave.
Wausau, WI 54401
<www.fiskars.com>
This company sells more than just scissors. Check out the online catalog for border cutters, photo corners, and stickers.

Frances Meyer, Inc.
(800) 372-6237
<www.francesmeyer.com>
Offers albums, papers, and more for heritage scrapbooks.

Generations Now
<www.generationsnow.com>
These memory products are considered safe for use in scrapbooks.

Gina Bear
P.O. Box 80406
Billings, MT 59108

K & Company
(800) 244-2083
<www.kandcompany.com>
Albums, papers, and specialty items.

Kodak
(800) 23KODAK
<www.kodak.com>
Contact for locations of the Picture Maker system.

Mrs. Grossman's Paper Co.
(800) 429-4549
<www.mrsgrossmans.com>
Look at the online catalog for listings of heritage album products.

Stampin' Up!
800-782-6787
<www.stampinup.com>
Papers, inks, and embossing powders.

Stewart Superior
2050 Farallon Dr.
San Leandro, CA 94577

3L Corp.
1120B Larkin Drive
Wheeling, IL 60090
(847) 808-1140
<www.3Lcorp.com>
Manufactures memorabilia pockets in a variety of sizes for including artifacts in your scrapbooks.

Un-du
Doumar Products, Inc.
(888) 289-8638
<www.un-du.com>

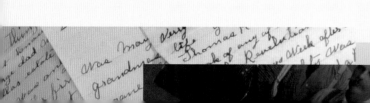

ARCHIVAL SUPPLIERS

American Institute for
Conservation of Historic & Artistic
Work, Inc. (AIC)
  Conservation Services Referral
  System
  1717 K. Street, NW Suite 200
  Washington, DC 20006
  (202) 452-9545
  <aic.stanford.edu>

Archival Products
  Des Moines, IA
  (800) 526-5640

Bags Unlimited
  Rochester, NY
  (800) 767-2247

Clear File, Inc.
  P.O. Box 593433
  Orlando, FL 32859
  (800) 423-0274

Conservation Center for Art &
Historic Artifacts (CCAHA)
  264 South 23rd St.
  Philadelphia, PA 19103
  (215) 545-0613

Conservation Materials Ltd.
  1165 Marietta Way
  P.O. Box 2884
  Sparks, NV 89431

Conservation Resources
  8000-H Forbes Place
  Springfield, VA 22151
  (800) 634-6932

Exposures
  Oshgosh, WI
  (800) 222-4927

Gaylord Bros.
  P.O. Box 4901
  Syracuse, NY 13221
  (800) 448-6160

Hollinger
  P.O. Box 6185
  Arlington, VA 22206
  (800) 634-0491

Hollinger Corporation
  P.O. Box 8360
  Fredericksburg, VA 22404
  (800) 634-0491

Icon Distribution
  Orlando, FL
  (800) 801-2128

Light Impressions
  P.O. Box 787
  Brea, CA 92822
  (800) 828-6216
  <www.lightimpressionsdirect.
  com>

Metal Edge
  Los Angeles, CA
  (800) 862-2228

Northeast Document Conservation
Center (NEDCC)
  100 Brickstone Square
  Andover, MA 01810
  (508) 470-1010

Ocker & Trapp
  17c Palisade Avenue
  Emerson, NJ 07630

Paige Co.
  Fort Lee, NJ
  (800) 957-2443

University Products
  517 Main St.
  P.O. Box 101
  Holyoke, MA 01041
  (800) 762-1165
  Conservation help.

University Products/The Archival
Company
  517 Main St.
  P.O. Box 101
  Holyoke, MA 01041
  (800) 628-1912

ORGANIZATIONS AND LIBRARIES

Allen County Public Library
900 Webster St.
Box 2270
Fort Wayne, IN 46801
(260) 421-1200
<www.acpl.lib.in.us>
Like most large research
libraries, Allen County Public
Library has a special department devoted to art research.

American Antiquarian Society
185 Salisbury St.
Worcester, Massachusetts 01609
(508) 755-5221
<www.americanantiquarian.
org>
Search the online guide to collections. Among its strengths
are eighteenth- and nineteenth-
century engravings. Researchers
must apply to use the collection.

American Printing History
Association
Box 4922
Grand Central Station
New York, NY 10163
<www.printinghistory.org>
The American Printing History
Association promotes the study
of the history of printing.

New England Historic Genealogical
Society
101 Newbury St.
Boston, MA 02116
(617) 536-5740
<www.newenglandancestors.
org>
The oldest genealogical society
in the United States.

New York Public Library
Print Collection
Humanities and Social Sciences
Library
Fifth Avenue and 42nd St.
New York, NY 10018
(212) 930-0817
<www.nypl.org/research/chss/
spe/art/print/print.html>
Learn about the history of
printing and search the collec-
tion.

STATE HISTORICAL SOCIETIES ONLINE

This list focuses on historical societies that operate on a state-wide basis. Elizabeth Petty Bentley's The Genealogist's Address Book (Genealogical Publishing Company, 1998) and The Ancestry Family Historian's Address Book by Juliana Szucs Smith (Ancestry, 1998) should be consulted for mailing addresses as well as local historical and genealogical societies. This is what was available at the time of writing.

Alabama
Alabama Historical Association
• No contact information available at this time.

Alaska
Alaska Historical Society
<www.alaska.net/~ahs/>
• All-volunteer membership society.
• Send e-mail to ahs@aska.net.
• No genealogical information is available on the site, but there are links to other institutions.

Arizona
Arizona Historical Society
<www.ahs.state.az.us>
• Contact for information on their research policies.

Arkansas
Arkansas Historical Association
422 South Sixth St.
Van Buren, AK 72201
• No library or research staff.

California
California Historical Society
<www.calhist.org>
• Online catalog.
• Genealogists are directed to other organizations.

Colorado
Colorado Historical Society
<www.history.state.co.us>
• Online catalog.
• Research information.
• Explanation of research fees.
• Send e-mail to library@chs.state.co.us.

Connecticut
Connecticut Historical Society
<www.chs.org/library>
• State-wide online catalog.
• Research policy on site.
• Send e-mail requests to Judith_e_ Johnson@chs.org.

Delaware
Historical Society of Delaware
<www.hsd.org>
• A full online guide to genea-logical research at the historical society is available on its Web site.
• Click on "Comments and Questions" at the bottom of the page for a directory of e-mail addresses.

District of Columbia
Historical Society of Washington, DC
<www.hswdc.org>
• Site outlines research fees.
• Send e-mail to Library@hswdc.org.

Florida
Florida Historical Society
<www.florida-historical-soc.org/youfoundus.html>
• Join the Florida listserv of history and genealogy related topics by sending an e-mail to wynne@metrolink.net with the message "Subscribe."

Georgia
Georgia Historical Society
<www.georgiahistory.com>
• The staff does not undertake extensive genealogical research.
• A link to a list of county historians is provided.
• Partial list of manuscript inventories.

Hawaii
Hawaiian Historical Society
<www.hawaiianhistory.org>
• Limited amounts of research are available by mail.
• Write to the Society at 560 Kawaiahao Street, Honolulu, HI 96813

Idaho
Idaho State Historical Society
<www2.state.id.us/ishs/>
• Specific questions answered.
• Check its list of cemeteries, city directories, college and high school yearbooks, and census indexes before sending a request.
• Genealogical questions should be directed to Plyons@ishs.state.id.us.

Illinois

Illinois State Historical Society
<www.prairienet.org/ishs>
• No genealogical material available online via its site.
• Send e-mail to ishs@eosinc.com.

Indiana

Indiana Historical Society
<www.indianahistory.org>
• Staff undertakes limited requests (up to thirty minutes).
• Questions should be directed to Emundell@indianahistory.org.
• Site includes a list of independent researchers under "General Library Information."

Iowa

State Historical Society of Iowa
<www.iowahistory.org>
• Read the e-mail request policy under "Library Services" before contacting the society.

Kansas

Kansas State Historical Society
<www.kshs.org>
• An extensive list of its holdings for genealogists appears on its site.
• Contact Reference@kshs.org with questions regarding its resources.
• Staff does not answer research requests, but will direct your letter to an independent researcher.

Kentucky

Kentucky Historical Society
<www.state.ky.us/agencies/khs/>
• Submit a copy of the Library Reference Request Form available online for research inquiries.
• Online catalog.

Louisiana

Louisiana Historical Society
Maritime Building
New Orleans, LA 70130
• No Web site at this time.

Maine

Center for Maine History
<www.mainehistory.com/genealogy.html>
• Join its online genealogy forum.
• Read about its policies regarding research on this site.
• Printable five-generation chart.

Maryland

Maryland Historical Society
<www.mdhs.org>
• An overview of its genealogical material and services is listed on the Library page.
• Send requests to Library@mdhs.org.

Massachusetts

Massachusetts Historical Society
<www.masshist.org>
• Limited research will be conducted.
• Online catalog.

Michigan

Historical Society of Michigan
<www.hsofmich.org>
• There is no genealogical information published on the site.

Minnesota

Minnesota Historical Society
<www.mnhs.org>
• Access to an online card catalog helps you discover its genealogical resources.
• If you are unable to visit the library, independent researchers can consult the collections for you.
• Basic genealogical research techniques are explained for beginners.

Mississippi

Mississippi Historical Society
<www.mdah.state.ms.us/admin/mhistsoc.html>
• This site offers a short history of the society and membership information.

Missouri

State Historical Society of Missouri
<www.system.missouri.edu/shs>
• Features guides to Missouri research.
• Online card catalog (small percentage of the collection).

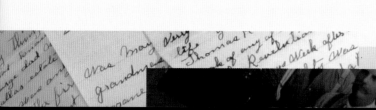

Montana

Montana Historical Society
<www.his.state.mt.us>
• Click on "Library" for a brief overview of the collections.
• No e-mail address for research requests.
• Two independent researchers listed on the site.

Nebraska

Nebraska State Historical Society
<www.nebraskahistory.org>
• Online guide for genealogical research at the Nebraska State Historical Society.
• Staff offers to do limited research for a fee.
• A helpful list of what the Society can do appears on the site under "Research/Resources" and then "Family History."
• Some materials available via interlibrary loan.

Nevada

Nevada Historical Society
<dmla.clan.lib.nv.us/docs/ museums/reno/his-soc.htm>
• Staff will assist in finding a professional researcher.
• Photocopying is done on a limited basis.

New Hampshire

New Hampshire Historical Society
<www.nhhistory.org>
• Staff charges for research.
• Search its online catalog before sending requests.
• Send e-mail to bcopeley@ nhhistory.org.

New Jersey

New Jersey State Historical Society
<www.jerseyhistory.org>
• Online guide to family history research.

New Mexico

Historical Society of New Mexico
P.O. Box 1912
Santa Fe, NM 87504-1912
• No Web site at this time.

New York

New-York Historical Society
<www.nyhistory.org>
• No explanation of resources for genealogists appears on the site.
• Send requests to the New-York Historical Society, 2 West 77th Street, New York, NY 10024.

North Carolina

Federation of North Carolina Historical Societies
109 East Jones St.
Raleigh, NC 27601-2807
• No Web site at this time.

North Dakota

State Historical Society of North Dakota
<www.state.nd.us/hist/>
• Become familiar with its genealogical research materials through an information sheet.
• Find individuals in the online index to the 1885 census for North Dakota.
• Access a complete list of North Dakota newspapers.

Ohio

Ohio Historical Society
<www.ohiohistory.org>
• Look at "Archives and Research Tools" to find a list of newspapers, the online catalog, and a database of death certificates from 1913-1937.
• Fill out a contact form for requests.

Oklahoma

Oklahoma Historical Society
<www.ok-history.mus.ok.us/>
• A list of research services and fees can be found by selecting "Library."
• The society suggests using its biography research form for inquiries.
• Only specific questions will be answered.

Oregon

Oregon Historical Society
<www.ohs.org>
• Click on "Collections" to find out more about resources for genealogy.
• Staff charges an hourly fee for research.
• Send requests to Orhist@ ohs.org.

Pennsylvania

Historical Society of Pennsylvania
<www.hsp.org/>
• Site features a group of specialized research guides of interest to family historians.
• The link to the society's research policies is conveniently located on the home page.

Rhode Island
Rhode Island Historical Society
<www.rihs.org>
• Contains basic information on the society's library.

South Carolina
South Carolina Historical Society
<www.schistory.org>
• Search the online surname database of more than sixty thousand names; send your questions regarding this resource to Info@schistory.org.

South Dakota
South Dakota State Historical Society
<www.state.sd.us/deca/cultural/sdshs.htm>
• Look under the "State Archives" link to find out how to request information or access the statewide library network.

Tennessee
Tennessee Historical Society
• Direct family history inquiries to the Tennessee State Library and Archives <www.state.tn.us/sos/statelib/tslahome.htm>.

Texas
Texas State Historical Association
• No genealogical information appears on this site.

Utah
Utah State Historical Society
300 Rio Grande Street
Salt Lake City, UT 84101
• Not able to open the site.

Vermont
Vermont Historical Society
<www.state.vt.us/vhs>
• Site features a guide to genealogical research in Vermont with links to organizations with URLs.
• Staff charges per twenty minutes of research.

Virginia
Virginia Historical Society
• Send requests to the Library, Virginia Historical Society, P.O. Box 7311, Richmond, VA 23221 with a check for twenty dollars to cover the maximum one hour of research.
• Site features a genealogy request form for individuals to use.
• The society does not accept fax or e-mail requests.

Washington
Washington State Historical Society
<www.wshs.org>
• No genealogical material available online.

West Virginia
West Virginia Historical Society
<www.wvculture.org/history/wvhssoc.html>
• This link lists articles that appeared in the society's quarterly magazine.

Wisconsin
State Historical Society of Wisconsin
<www.shsw.wisc.edu>
• Staff will answer requests for information; send requests to the State Historical Society of Wisconsin Library, 816 State Street, Madison, WI 53706.

Wyoming
Wyoming State Historical Society
<http://wyshs.org>
• No research policies online as of this writing.

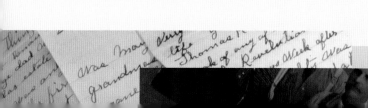

LOOK FOR THESE OTHER GREAT FAMILY HISTORY TITLES FROM BETTERWAY BOOKS!

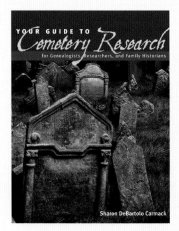

Cemeteries can help fill the holes in your precious family history! With this book, you'll learn how to determine when and where a person died, locate the exact cemetery in which a family or individual is interred, analyze headstones and markers, interpret funerary art and tombstone iconography, and more!

ISBN 1-55870-589-9, paperback, 192 pages, #70527-K

These books and other fine Betterway titles are available from your local bookstore, online supplier or by calling 1-800-448-0915.

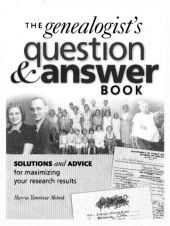

More than 150 answers to the most commonly asked questions are found here in a friendly, easy-to-browse format that will clarify the research process and save you time and confusion as you fill in your family tree. Questions are conveniently grouped according to the different resources you'll use: from census, church and immigration records to oral histories, Web sites, electronic databases and more.

ISBN 1-55870-590-2, paperback, 240 pages, #70528-K

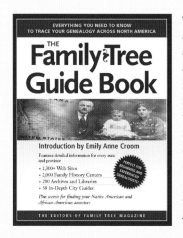

This invaluable resource - from the editors at Family Tree Magazine - combines genealogy basics, online directories and region-specific travel information in one book. Divided into 7 regions of the US with a chapter covering Canada, each section introduces you to a specific region and provides guidelines for finding and using its records.

ISBN 1-55870-647-X, paperback, 352 pages, #70595-K

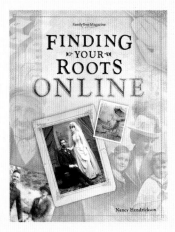

It's the guide you need to lead you through your online research! Nancy Hendrickson's structured, easy-to-follow approach covers the basics of sound genealogical research, then helps you navigate the Internet, efficiently and effectively. Also included are pages of tips and techniques for organizing computer research that can make your online efforts easier, faster and more productive.

ISBN 1-55870-635-6, paperback, 240 pages, #70583-K

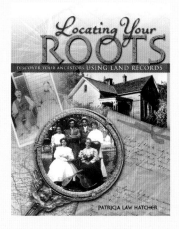

Acclaimed genealogist Patricia Law Hatcher gives you easy-to-follow instructions for identifying, finding and interpreting the most common types of land records. She also includes in-depth advice for finding a deed in a courthouse, recording what you find and figuring out how land was transferred. Add to your deed research and land-platting efforts with more than 50 illustrations, maps and atlases which are also included.

ISBN 1-55870-614-3, paperback, 240 pages, #70556-K

EXPLORE THE WORLD OF SCRAPBOOKING!

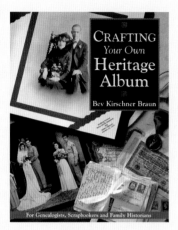

This guide helps you capture and pre-serve the precious keepsakes of your family history. You'll learn to create an elegant album that weaves family his-tory, lore and tradition with cherished photos, documents and memorabilia and preserves them for generations to come!

ISBN 1-55870-534-1, paperback, 128 pages, #70457-K

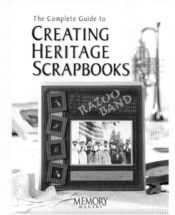

Learn to preserve precious family memories in a one-of-a-kind heritage album. This books guides you through the process of researching family history, protecting old photos & memorabilia, and creating stunning scrapbooks that are sure to become family treasures.

ISBN 1-892127-22-9, paperback, 128 pages, #32473-K

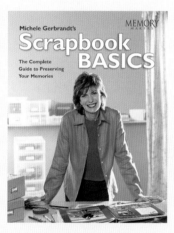

This book provides all the informa-tion you need to create your own scrapbooks with confidence! You'll learn how to select the most useful starter supplies, organize photos and negatives and set up an efficient workspace while finding tips on designing page layouts, cropping pho-tos, adding journal entries, and more.

ISBN 1-892127-16-4, paperback, 128 pages, #32417-K

Enrich your pages and by combining two pastimes both personal and long lasting - writing and scrapbooking. Inside are stunning color photos that instruct and inspire scrapbookers to create pages which will speak to gen-erations to come. Tips on what to say and how to say it, lists of powerful, descriptive words, advice for over-coming journaling jitters and much more also included.

ISBN 1-892127-23-7, paperback, 96 pages, #32459-K

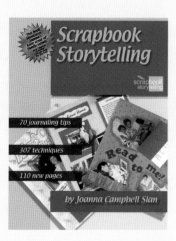

Go beyond typical scrapbooking tech-niques! This inspiring book offers dozens of great ideas for documenting family stories and events with words and images. You'll find step-by-step techniques for creating clever scrap-book layouts and unique booklets - even web pages! You'll also learn new ways to combine cherished family sto-ries with photos, collages and illustra-tions.

ISBN 0-9630222-8-8, paperback, 144 pages, #70450-K

These books and other fine North Light tiles are available from your local art & craft retailer, bookstore, online supplier or by calling 1-800-448-0915.

LOOK FOR THESE VIDEOS FROM FAMILY HISTORY EXPERT MAUREEN TAYLOR!

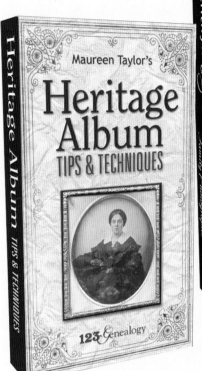

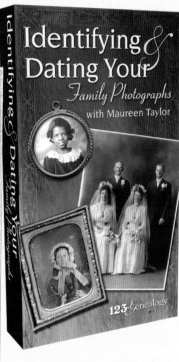

IDENTIFYING & DATING YOUR FAMILY PHOTOGRAPHS

When's the last time you looked at your family photographs? If you're like most people you've spent countless hours looking through shoeboxes of images, but don't know how to tell the story of your pictures or how to identify unnamed portraits.

In this video Maureen, The Photo Detective, will teach you how to examine your pictures and discover more about your family history by uncovering the stories and time periods relating to those precious family treasures.
She also explains how to:

• Identify and organize your family photographs
• Identify types of photographs
• Date an image by identifying the costume and styles
• Preserve original family photographs
• Find pictures of each person on your family tree from 1839 to the present
• Identify your unidentified pictures
• Share pictures with relatives
• Select digital solutions for organizing your photographs

$19.95, ISBN 1-58629-136-X, UPC 683275052839, VHS video 75 minutes

HERITAGE ALBUM TIPS AND TECHNIQUES

Maureen offers unique tips and techniques for building historically accurate and visually appealing heritage albums including how to:

• Trace your family tree
• Create a sense of history in your albums
• Locate new materials such as photographs, documents, memorabilia and artifacts to include in a heritage album
• Create a sense of history in your albums
• Use safe scrapbooking methods to preserve your pages for generations to come
• Choose digital solutions including photo editing software and the Internet
• Identify your family photographs
• Produce creative heritage albums that express your family history

Maureen also provides examples that you can duplicate in your own heritage albums. So get started today!

$19.95, ISBN 1-58629-135-1 , UPC 683275052631, VHS video 55 minutes